The Architect, or Practical House Carpenter (1830)

by Asher Benjamin

DOVER PUBLICATIONS, INC., *New York*

This Dover edition, first published in 1988, is an unabridged republication of the work that first appeared in 1830. The present edition, to achieve the best results in reproduction (etc.), uses pages from two subsequent reprints, one published by L. Coffin, Boston, 1844, and the other published by Benjamin B. Mussey & Co., Boston, 1850. Both reprints had a title page reading: "The / Architect, / or / Practical House Carpenter; / illustrated by / sixty-four engravings, / which exhibit the orders of architecture, / and / other elements of the art; / designed / for the use of carpenters and builders." Some of the plates have been moved from their original locations. Older or odder spelling variants such as "frize" and "pannel" have been left unaltered.

Manufactured in the United States of America
Dover Publications, Inc., 31 East 2nd Street, Mineola, N.Y. 11501

Library of Congress Cataloging-in-Publication Data

Benjamin, Asher, 1773–1845.
  The architect, or, Practical house carpenter.

  Reprint. Originally published: Boston : L. Coffin, 1844.
  1. Greek revival (Architecture)—Designs and plans. I. Title.
II. Title: Architect.   III. Title: Practical house carpenter.
NA600.B46 1988   721′.3   88-18105
ISBN 0-486-25802-5 (pbk.)

PREFACE.

THE favorable manner in which my former publications on Architecture have been received, and the want of a practical treatise on that subject, adapted to the present style of building in our own country, are the principal motives which induce me to place this work before the public.

Since my last publication, the Roman school of architecture has been entirely changed for the Grecian. Very few things of the same nature differ more than the Greek and Roman creeds of the orders. The Roman orders are chiefly composed of small and ungraceful parts, and the mouldings are made up of parts of a circle, which do not produce that beautiful light and shade, so happily effected by the Grecian mouldings. These latter are composed of parts of ellipses, parabolas, hyperbolas and other conic sections, and consist, mostly, of large, bold parts, which are so strongly marked, that each member of the profile is plainly seen at a very considerable distance; and can likewise be executed with less expense than the former. I confess myself to be an admirer of Grecian architecture, yet I am not disposed to condemn the general proportions of the Roman orders, none of which, except the Doric, differ essentially from those of the Grecian. The column of that order was generally made, by the Greeks, about five diameters in height; but the same order was generally made, by the Romans, from seven and a half to eight diameters in height. It is therefore evident that the latter proportion comes nearer to our practice than the former one, especially when the orders are used in private houses. The members of the Grecian columns and entablatures, however, are certainly better proportioned to each other than those of the Roman.

With a strong desire to make this work useful to the practical builder, I have endeavored to divest myself of any prejudice I might have for or against any school of architecture, and to select, from all the books on that subject, those parts which I thought would best promote my object. With this view, I have first given an example of the Tuscan order, which is of Roman origin; then one of the Doric order, from the Temple of Theseus at Athens, exactly corresponding to the measures taken of that celebrated building by Stuart and Revet; again, a second example of the Doric order, from Sir William Chambers, whose orders are esteemed the most perfect and beautiful of the Roman school; and lastly, a third example, composed from the two first, but chiefly from the Temple of Theseus, which I believe better adapted to the practice of our own country, at the present time, than either of the others,—but those who differ from me in opinion have one of the most perfect of the Greek, and one of the best of the Roman examples, to make their selection from. I have proceeded in the same manner with the Ionic orders, giving first an example from the Temple of Minerva

Polias at Priene, which is considered one of the best Greek examples; secondly, an example from Sir William Chambers; and thirdly, one of my own compiling, which is chiefly Greek, the capital being taken from the Ionic temple on the river Illyssus at Athens. The Corinthian order having been little used by the Greeks, the Roman examples are generally esteemed the most perfect; I have therefore given an example of this order from the Temple of Jupiter Stator at Rome. Although the Composite order was evidently of Roman origin, and is not much in use here or elsewhere, I have nevertheless thought it proper to give an elevation of that order from that most beautiful example, the Arch of Titus at Rome. I have also given a profile of the entablature and capital, taken from the Choragic Monument of Thrasyllus at Athens, and the Ionic entablature from the Temple of the Muses, at the same place; and also several other examples for entablatures and capitals, which will often be found useful.

I consider it necessary that all practical house carpenters should be fully acquainted with the orders of architecture, particularly those who reside in the country, where they have no opportunity of consulting an architect: I have therefore been very particular in the descriptive part of the orders; which care, together with that I have taken in drawing and representing the most difficult parts on a large scale, will, I am persuaded, make them so plain and easy, that a workman of ordinary capacity can make himself perfect master of the orders, without the aid of an instructer; and when he fully comprehends them, he will be able to understand the whole subject of this book.

With a view to render this work completely a practical one, and to facilitate and assist the efforts of master carpenters, I have drawn all the architraves, base and sur-base mouldings, and all other examples where it was possible so to do, at full size for practice, and I trust they will be found particularly useful to those carpenters who have not had an opportunity of learning to draw architectural subjects.

I am indebted to **Mr. Peter Nicholson's** ingenious treatise on stairs for the principles of handrailing. I have made the drawings on that subject somewhat different from his, and have explained them in my own way. I therefore believe that this book will be found to contain the most direct and best method of handrailing, and will, I am persuaded, be more useful to the stair builder than any one of his books on that subject.

Three editions of this work, each containing one thousand copies, having been sold, the author is encouraged to publish a fourth. He acknowledges his gratitude to the public for their liberal patronage, and hopes the work will still be found useful to them.

A. BENJAMIN.

INDEX.

———

PRACTICAL HOUSE CARPENTER.

PRACTICAL GEOMETRY.

PLATE I.

FIG. 1.

In a given square, A B C D, to describe a regular octagon. With one half the distance A C or B D, and on A B C D, as centres, describe the arcs *g m d, e m k, c m h*, and *f m i;* join *f e, d c, k i,* and *h g*, and it will be the octagon required.

FIG. 2

In a given circle to describe an equilateral triangle. Upon any point, A, in the circumference, with the radius A G, describe the arc B G F; draw B F, and make B D equal to B F; join D F and D B, then B D F will be the equilateral triangle required.

FIG. 3

In a given circle to describe a square or an octagon. Draw the diameter A C and B D at right angles; join A B, B C, C D and D A, and A B C D will be the square. For the octagon, bisect A B in E, and carry A E eight times around the circumference.

FIG. 4, 5 and 6.

Upon a given line, *a b*, to construct any regular polygon. Upon *a* and *b* as centres, with a radius equal to *a b*, describe two arcs in tersecting each other at f; from b draw the perpendicular $b\ c$, and divide the arc $a\ c$ into as many equal parts as the polygon is to have sides. Through the second division d draw $b\ g$; make $e\ f$ equal to $f\ d$, and through e draw $a\ g$, meeting $b\ g$ at g; then g will be the centre, and $g\ a$ the radius of a circle, that will contain $a\ b$ to any number of sides required.

FIG. 7.

To describe the segment of a circle by means of a triangle. Let $A\ B$ be the length of the segment, and $C\ D$ the perpendicular height in the middle; through the points D and A draw $D\ A$, and draw $D\ E$ parallel to $A\ B$; make $D\ E$ equal to $D\ A$, and join $E\ A$, which makes the triangle $E\ D\ A$. Put in pins at the points $A\ D\ B$; then move your triangle around the points D and A, and the angular point will describe half the segment. The other half will be described in the same manner, which will complete the whole segment required.

FIG. 8.

The transverse and conjugate axes $A\ B$ and $C\ D$ of an ellipsis being given, to find the two foci, and from thence to describe an ellipsis. Take the semitransverse $A\ E$ or $E\ B$, and from C as a centre describe an arc cutting $A\ B$ at F and G, which will be the foci.

Fix pins in those points, a string being extended about the points $F\ C\ G$, then move the point C around the fixed points F and G, keeping the string tight, and the ellipsis will be described.

FIG. 9.

To describe an ellipsis by an instrument called a trammel. Set the distance of the first pin, B, from the pencil at C, to half the shortest diameter, and the distance of the second pin, A, to half the longest diameter; the pins being put in the grooves, as shown in the figure; then move the pencil at C, and it will describe the ellipsis required.

MOULDINGS.

PLATE II.

FIG. 1, 2 and 3.

To describe the Grecian echinus, or ovolo to any given height and projection.   Figures 1, 2 and 3 are all of one height, but of different projections.   Divide their heights (excluding the quick) and their projections, each into a like number of equal parts; through the divisions 1 2 3 and 4, on the line of height, draw lines parallel to the moulding, and also from A, at the extremity of the outline, draw lines to 1 2 3 and 4, on the line of projection; then through the points, where these lines cut those first described, trace the outline of the echinus, and continue it as judgment directs from A around the quick to the fillet.   The outline just described is a parabola, and that of fig. 4 is an hyperbola, which may be drawn by leaving off the lower fourth part, or more or less of the line of height A D; or, which produces the same thing, from the points on the line of height at C, draw lines which, if produced, would meet in a point at a distance of once or twice the projection of the moulding, or more or less, remembering that the nearer the moulding these lines meet, the nearer will the outline of the echinus approach to a straight line.

It will be plainly seen, that, by the application of the conic sections either to the echinus cimarecta or cimareversa, an endless variety of beautiful outlines may be obtained.

To describe the cimareversa, fig. 5, divide A B and 3 D each into a like number of equal parts, into six for instance, as here, and draw A 1, A 2, A 3, and C 1, C 2, C 3; then trace the curve as before directed.

To describe a scotia, fig. 6, join the ends of each fillet by the right line **A B**; bisect **A B** at **D**; through **D** draw **C D F** parallel to the fillets, and **C D** and **D F**, each equal to the depth of the scotia; divide **D A, D B, A G** and **B F**, each into the same number of equal parts; from **E**, and through **1 2 3** on **A G**, and also through **1 2 3** on **B F**, draw lines. Then, from the point **C**, and through the points **1 2 3** on the line **A B**, draw lines, cutting the former lines at **1 2 3 4 5 6**, and trace the curve through those points.

TUSCAN ORDER.

PLATE III.

THE Tuscan order is nearly the same in its proportions as the Doric. Of this order we have no complete example remaining from antique buildings. There is one given by Vitruvius, from whom we derive all we know concerning the origin of the order, of which the column is seven diameters high, including base and capital, and diminishes one fourth part of its lower diameter. But the cornice projects more than one fourth part of the height of the column, which renders the example unfit for our practice.

In the example here given, I have, in imitation of Vitruvius, made the column seven diameters high, including base and capital, and the entablature two diameters; although in practice I do not always follow this rule, since, in different situations, both column and entablature require different proportions. They should in all cases be proportioned according to the weight, or apparent weight, which they have to sustain. It will sometimes be convenient to lower the entablature, in which case it may be reduced to one hundred and ten minutes, **or** any where between one hundred and ten and one hundred and twenty, taken in about equal proportions from the frieze and architrave, and leaving the cornice its full proportions. The base given in this example may, when expense is to be avoided, be kept off with propriety; and particularly when the column is seven diameters or less. The mouldings in the capital and cornice are Grecian, although the order is of Roman origin.

To draw the Tuscan order to any given height, the height given must be divided into nine equal parts, because, the column being seven and the entablature two diameters, one ninth of the height is the diameter of the column just above the base. Suppose it be required to find the diameter of the column to a height of twenty-one feet. One ninth of twenty-one feet is two feet four inches. Of that length make a scale of sixty equal parts, which are called minutes. First divide two feet four inches into six equal parts, like the scale *a b;* then divide *a* 10 into two equal parts, and *a* 5 into five parts. Each of the last divisions will be one minute, or a sixtieth part of the diameter of the column.

Under **H** and against each member of the order is figured the number of minutes in their respective heights, and under **P**, the number of minutes which each member projects. The measures of the order are to be taken from the scale of minutes above, as will be seen by the following directions given for drawing the base. Against the plinth *c d* is fifteen minutes; take fifteen minutes from your scale, and set it down on a vertical line drawn for the side of the column. Against the torus is twelve minutes; set that down on the same line; and against the fillet *e f* is three minutes; set that down also. Under **P** and against the plinth at *g* is ten minutes, the projection of the plinth; set that down at right angles with the column, and draw the line *g* across the plinth. Against the torus at *h* is ten minutes, its projection; with six minutes in your compasses describe the half circle, which completes the torus. Against the fillet at *i* is four minutes, which set off for its projection; then, with four and a half minutes in your compasses, describe the part of a circle which joins the fillet to the column, and the base is completed. Go on in the same way to describe the remaining part of the order.

A is a section of the cornice showing the bedmould recessed up into the soffit of the corona.

B is a section of the band to the architrave.

C is the capital drawn on a large scale for the purpose of showing the exact curve of the ovolo.

GRECIAN DORIC ORDER.

PLATE IV.

FIG. 1.

THE district of Argolis first received colonies who introduced civilization into Greece. It has been reckoned the cradle of the Greeks, the theatre of the events which produced their earliest annals, and the country which produced their first heroes and artists. It was in the temple of Juno at Argos, where the Doric order first arose to a marked eminence, and became the model for the magnificent edifices afterwards erected in the other cities, states, and islands. After the Doric order had been established in the temple of Juno at Argos, it was employed in the temple of Jupiter Nemeus, between Argos and Corinth; Jupiter Olympius, at Olympia in Elis; in a splendid triple portico in the city of Elis; and also in three temples in the same city, to Juno, Minerva, and Dindymene; at Eleusis, in the great temple to Ceres; in that of Minerva, at Sunium; in the temple of Minerva Parthenon; in the temple of Theseus; in the entrance to the Acropolis, and other public edifices, of great magnitude and splendor, at Athens. In many of the islands there were also temples of the Doric model; that of Apollo in the isle of Delos; Juno in Samos; Jupiter Panellenius, Ægina, and Silenus, in Sicily; and innumerable in places of inferior note. Even in Ionia, it was employed in the temple of Apollo Panionius. Many of these edifices were of great magnitude. The temples of the Greeks were universally of an oblong form; in some, the porticos were at the ends only; in others, they were extended quite around the cell, some in single, others in double ranges; some were covered with roofs, others were left partly uncovered; and some of them were divided by ranges of pillars along the middle of the cell. The superstructure was placed upon a platform composed of three steps, which surrounded the whole edifice, and upon which the columns were all placed without bases. The number of columns was either six along the ends and thirteen along the sides, or eight along the ends and seventeen along the sides, counting the angular columns twice. When formed upon so large a scale and the ranges of columns so distinctly insulated, and when artists of the first talents not only formed the models of the edifice, and directed its execution, but also, under the strongest influence of rivalship and thirst of glory, with their own hands clothed those edifices with sculptures, and enriched them with statues, under these circumstances the essential parts of the Doric order produced effects not to be exceeded for simplicity and majesty.

That the proportion which the different members of the Doric order bore to each other was practised by the Greeks with considerable latitude, and that the ancients did not scrupulously adhere to any precise proportion, will be evident from the following table, which exhibits the dimensions of the principal parts of this order in many of the ancient Greek edifices, which have been examined with accuracy. The dimensions here put down are in diameters and minutes.

A Table of the Proportions of the Doric Order of Architecture.

Names of Examples.	Bottom Diameter.	Top Diameter.	Height of Column.		Architrave.	Frieze.	Cornice.	Intercolumniation.	
	Min.	Min.	Diam.	Min.	Min.	Min.	Min.	Diam.	Min.
Portico of the Agora, at Athens . .	60	47	6	$2\frac{1}{2}$	40	42	21	——	——*
Temple of Minerva, at Sunium . .	60	$45\frac{3}{4}$	5	54	$48\frac{1}{2}$	$48\frac{1}{2}$	——	1	28
Temple of Jupiter Nemæus . . .	60	49	6	31	$38\frac{2}{3}$	$43\frac{1}{2}$	——	——	——
Temple of Jupiter Panellenius . .	60	$44\frac{1}{2}$	5	24	$51\frac{1}{3}$	$51\frac{1}{2}$	——	1	41
Temple of Theseus.	60	$46\frac{2}{3}$	5	$42\frac{1}{3}$	50	$49\frac{1}{2}$	——	1	$37\frac{1}{2}$
Temple of Minerva, at Athens . .	60	47	5	$33\frac{1}{2}$	43	43	32	1	$17\frac{2}{3}$
Temple at Corinth	60	$44\frac{2}{3}$	4	4	$48\frac{2}{3}$	——	——	1	14
Portico of Philip	60	$49\frac{1}{2}$	6	$32\frac{1}{2}$	$38\frac{1}{2}$	$43\frac{3}{4}$	$25\frac{1}{2}$	2	$42\frac{2}{3}$
Temple of Apollo	60	$42\frac{1}{2}$	6	$3\frac{3}{4}$	$49\frac{2}{3}$	$42\frac{1}{2}$	——	——	——
Temple of Minerva, at Syracuse . .	60	46	4	$24\frac{1}{2}$	$44\frac{1}{2}$	40	——	1	$5\frac{2}{3}$
Temple of Juna Lucina	60	$45\frac{1}{3}$	4	42	55	45	——	1	15
Temple of Concord	60	46	4	$45\frac{1}{4}$	$46\frac{4}{5}$	$46\frac{1}{3}$	25	1	$10\frac{2}{3}$
Pseudo-Dipteral Temple, at Pæstum	60	$40\frac{1}{3}$	4	27	50	——	——	1	$7\frac{1}{3}$
Hexastyle Temple, at Pæstum . .	60	43	4	$47\frac{3}{4}$	$45\frac{3}{4}$	$44\frac{3}{4}$	$24\frac{3}{4}$	1	$1\frac{1}{3}$
Hypaethral Temple, at Pæstum . .	60	$41\frac{1}{4}$	4	8	$42\frac{1}{3}$	$40\frac{1}{2}$	$21\frac{1}{2}$	1	$4\frac{3}{4}$
Inner Peristyle of ditto	60	43	4	$13\frac{1}{3}$	39	——	——	1	$22\frac{3}{4}$
Upper columns of ditto, ditto . .	60	$44\frac{1}{3}$	3	50	68	——	——	2	49
Temple at Selinus.	60	46	4	$21\frac{3}{4}$	$46\frac{1}{3}$	$44\frac{2}{3}$	——	1	$2\frac{1}{3}$
Temple of Jupiter, at Selinus . . .	60	$35\frac{1}{2}$	4	$34\frac{1}{3}$	52	$44\frac{2}{3}$	26	——	——
Temple at Ægesta	60	$44\frac{3}{4}$	——	——	$49\frac{3}{4}$	$52\frac{2}{3}$	$40\frac{3}{4}$	1	11
Theatre of Marcellus	60	48	7	$51\frac{2}{3}$	30	$45\frac{5}{8}$	$57\frac{2}{7}$	——	——

In every Greek Doric, the vertical face of the architrave projects beyond the inferior diameter, but is within the superior one. In the

* Where the members have not been measured, they are noted in the table by this mark, ——.

temple of Corinth, and the Doric portico at Athens, the ovolo or echinus is of an elliptical shape; but in every other instance of Greek capitals, it is hyperbolical, excepting the single instance of the portico of Philip, king of Macedon, which is a straight line.

The number of annulets in the capital varies from three to five; and the number of horizontal grooves which separate the shaft from the capital varies from one to three.

Elevation of the Doric Order on the Temple of Theseus at Athens.

This temple is one of the most ancient and beautiful examples of that order now existing. It was erected about ten years after the battle of Salamis, by Cimon, the son of Miltiades. The ceiling of the porch is remarkable for its construction, having large beams of marble with the upper sides level with the bed of the cornice, and the ends corresponding exactly to the triglyphs in the frieze, which gives the idea of the disposition of the timbers first used in buildings, and from which the Doric order had its origin. This building is adorned with beautiful sculpture. The metopes of the frieze are charged with historical figures, in which are represented various exploits of Theseus.

The height of the column is five diameters and forty-two and a half minutes, and that of the entablature two diameters and ten minutes, so that column and entablature, both together, are seven diameters and fifty-two and a half minutes. If the column was seven and a half minutes higher than it is, its diameter would be one eighth part of the entire height; and it will be near enough in practice to divide the whole height into eight parts; then, giving one part to the diameter of the column, proceed to draw it as before directed in the

Tuscan order. The column diminishes thirteen minutes, and its sides are composed of straight lines or those gently curved.

Fig. 2 is a plan of the soffit inverted, showing the distribution of the drops, which are two and a half minutes in diameter, and one and a half in length.

Fig. 3 is a section of the cymatium on a large scale.

Fig. 4 shows the capital on a large scale, in which the cantor of the ovolo, and also the shape of the annulets, are more plainly seen.

ROMAN DORIC ORDER.

Doric Order, as approved by Sir William Chambers.

" Vignola's Doric being composed in a greater style, and in a manner more characteristic of the order, than any other, I have chosen it for my model; though, in particular members, I have not scrupled to vary, when observation taught me they might be improved.

" Perfect proportion, in architecture, if considered only with regard to the relations between the different objects in the composition, and as it merely relates to the pleasure of the sight, seems to consist in this; that those parts which are either principal or essential, should be contrived to catch the eye successively, from the most considerable to the least, according to their degrees of importance in the composition, and impress their images on the mind, before it is affected by any of the subservient members; yet, that these should be so conditioned, as not to be entirely absorbed, but be capable of raising distinct ideas likewise, and such as may be adequate to the purposes for which these parts are designed.

" The different figures and situations of the parts may, in some degree, contribute to this effect; for simple forms will operate more speedily than those that are complicated, and such as project will be sooner perceived than such as are more retired; but dimension seems to be the predominant quality, or that which acts most powerfully on the sense; and this, it is apprehended, can only be discovered by experience; at least to any degree of accuracy. When, therefore, a number of parts, arranged in a particular manner, and under particular dimensions, excite, in the generality of judicious spectators, a pleasing sensation, it will be prudent, on every occasion where the same circumstances subsist, to observe exactly the same arrangement and proportions; notwithstanding they may in themselves appear irregular, and unconnected.

" In composing the orders and other decorations which are contained in the present publication, this method has constantly been observed; the author having himself, with that view, measured with the utmost accuracy, and not without some danger, many ancient and modern celebrated buildings, both at Rome and in other parts of Europe; strictly copying such things as appeared to be perfect, and carefully correcting others, which seemed in any degree faulty, relying therein not alone on his own judgment, in doubtful cases, but much on the opinion and advice of several learned, ingenious artists of different nations, with whom he had the advantage of being intimately connected when abroad.

" The height of the Doric column, including its capital and base, is sixteen modules; and the height of the entablature, four modules; the latter of which being divided into eight parts, two of them are given to the architrave, three to the frieze, and the remaining three to the cornice.

" In most of the antiques, the Doric column is executed without a base; Vitruvius likewise makes it without one, the base, according to that author, having been first employed in the Ionic order, to imitate the sandal or covering to a woman's foot. Scammozzi blames this practice; and most of the moderns have been of his opinion, the greatest part of them having employed the Attic base in this order. Monsieur de Chambray, however, whose blind attachment to the antique is, on many occasions, sufficiently evident, argues vehemently against this practice, which, as the order is formed upon the model of a strong man, who is constantly represented barefooted, is, according to him, very improper; and 'though,' says he, 'the custom of employing a base, in contempt of all ancient authority, has, by some unaccountable and false notions of beauty, prevailed, yet, I doubt not but the purer eye, when apprized of this error, will easily be undeceived; and as what is merely plausible will, when examined, appear to be false, so apparent beauties, when not founded in reason, will of course be deemed extravagant.'

"In imitation of Palladio, and all the modern architects except Vignola, I have made use of the Attic base in this order: and it certainly is the most beautiful of any; though, for variety's sake, when the Doric and Ionic orders are employed together, the base invented by Vignola, of which a profile is annexed, may sometimes be used. Bernini has employed it in the colonnades of St. Peter's, and it has been successfully applied in many other buildings.

"The ancients sometimes made the shafts of the Doric column prismatic, as appears by a passage in the fourth book of Vitruvius: and at other times they adorned it with a particular kind of shallow flutings, described from the centre of a square, no interval or fillet being left between them. Of this sort there are now some columns to be seen in the temples of Pestum, near Naples; in different parts of Sicily; and in the church of St. Peter in Catenis, at Rome.

"Vitruvius gives to the height of the Doric capital one module; and all the moderns, except Alberti, have followed his example. Nevertheless, as it is of the same kind with the Tuscan, they should both bear nearly the same proportion to the heights of their respective columns; and, consequently, the Doric capital ought to be more than one module, which it accordingly is, both at the Coliseum and in the theatre of Marcellus; being, in the former of these buildings, upwards of thirty-eight minutes, and in the latter, thirty-three minutes high.

"In the design here offered, I have made the height of the whole capital thirty-two minutes, and, in the form and dimensions of the particular members, I have deviated but little from the profile of the theatre of Marcellus. The frieze or neck is enriched with husks and roses,* as in Palladio's design, and as it has been executed by Sangallo at the Farnese palace in Rome, and by Cigoli in the Cortile of the Strozzi at Florence, as well as in several buildings of note in this metropolis. The projection of these husks and flowers must not exceed that of the upper cincture of the column.

"The architrave is one module in height, and composed only of one fascia and a fillet, as at the theatre of Marcellus; the drops are conical, as they are in all the antiques; not pyramidal, as they are improperly made by most of our English workmen; they are supposed to represent drops of water draining from the triglyph, and, consequently, they should be cones, or parts of cones, not pyramids.

"The frieze and the cornice are each of them one module and a half in height; the metope is square, and enriched with a bull's scull, adorned with garlands of beads, in imitation of those on the temple of Jupiter Tonans, at the foot of the capital. In some antique fragments, and in

* The husks, roses and ox sculls, are left off in this example.

a greater number of modern buildings, the metopes are alternately enriched with these ox sculls, and with pateras; but they may be filled with any other ornaments of good forms, and frequently with greater propriety.

"Thus, in military structures, heads of Medusa, or of the Furies, thunderbolts, and other symbols of horror, may be introduced; likewise helmets, daggers, garlands of laurel or oak, and crowns of various kinds, such as those used among the Romans, and given as rewards for different military achievements; but spears, swords, quivers, bows, cuirasses, shields and the like, must be avoided, because the real dimensions of these things are too considerable to find admittance in such small compartments; and representations in miniature always carry with them an idea of triviality, carefully to be avoided in architecture, as in all other arts. In sacred buildings, cherubs, chalices, and garlands of palm or olive, may be employed; likewise doves, or other symbols of moral virtues. And in private houses, crests or badges of dignity may sometimes be suffered, though seldom, and indeed never, when they are of stiff, insipid forms.

"Too much variety in the ornaments of the metopes must be avoided, lest the unity of the composition should be destroyed. It is best never to introduce more than two different representations, which should not consist of above one, or at most two objects each, of simple forms, and not overcharged with ornaments. In the disposition of these, care must be taken to place them with regard to symmetry; those on the right in correspondence with those on the left. Wherefore, when a triglyph happens to be in the middle of a front, it becomes necessary to couple the middle ones, by filling the two metopes, on each side of the central triglyph, with the same sort of ornaments; distributing the rest alternately as usual. It is likewise to be observed, that ornaments in metopes are not to project beyond the triglyphs, which ought to predominate, as being essential and principal parts in the composition. Palladio, in his Basilica of Vicenza, has given to the most elevated part of the ox sculls and pateras, with which the metopes are filled, very little more projection than that of the triglyph; and in this he has copied the ancients, who seldom or never gave more projection to any ornament, than that of the frame or border in which it was enclosed; as appears by those inimitable fragments in the Villa Medici, and many others in different parts of Rome, and elsewhere. The channels of the triglyph, on their plan, commonly form a right angle; but, to give them more effect, a narrow square groove may be cut in the inner angle, from top to bottom, and into the solid of the frieze.

" In the cornice, I have deviated very little from my original. Le Clerc, who, in his Doric profile, has imitated that of Vignola, makes the mutules as broad as the capital of the triglyph. But Vignola's method is preferable, who makes them no broader than the triglyph: as it is more sightly and more conformable to the carpenter's art, in which the width of the rafter never exceeds the width of the beam or joist it stands upon. The ornaments of the soffit are nearly the same as those of Vignola. They should be entirely sunk up, wrought in the solid of the corona, and never drop down lower than its soffit. There is no necessity for cutting them deep: in most of Palladio's buildings, they do not enter above two minutes into the corona, and that is quite sufficient.

" Of all the entablatures, the Doric is most difficult to distribute, on account of the large intervals between the centres of the triglyphs, which neither admit of increase or diminution, without injuring the symmetry and regular beauty of the composition. These constant-

ly confine the composer to intercolumniations, divisible by two modules and a half, entirely exclude coupled columns, and produce
spaces which, in general, are either too wide or too narrow for his
purposes.

" To obviate these difficulties, the triglyphs have often been omitted, and the entablature made plain, as at the Coliseum in Rome,
the colonnades of St. Peter's, of the Vatican, and in many other
buildings both at home and abroad. This, indeed, is an easy expedient; but, while it robs the order of its principal characteristic distinction, leaves it poor, and very little superior to the Tuscan. The
remedy seems desperate, and should never be employed but as a last
resource.

" The ancients employed the Doric in temples dedicated to Minerva, to Mars, and to Hercules, whose grave and manly dispositions
suited well with the character of this order. Serlio says it is proper
for churches dedicated to Jesus Christ, to St. Paul, St. Peter, or
any other saints remarkable for their fortitude in exposing their
lives, and suffering for the Christian faith. Le Clerc recommends
the use of it in all kinds of military buildings, as arsenals, gates of
fortified places, guard-rooms, and similar structures. It may likewise
be employed in the houses of generals, or other martial men, in mau-
soleums erected to their memory, or in triumphal bridges and arches,
built to celebrate their victories.

" I have made the height of the Doric column sixteen modules;
which, in buildings where majesty or grandeur are required, is a
proper proportion; but in others, it may be somewhat more slender.
Thus Vitruvius makes the Doric column in porticos higher by half
a diameter than in temples; and most of the modern architects have,
on some occasions, followed his example. In private houses, there-

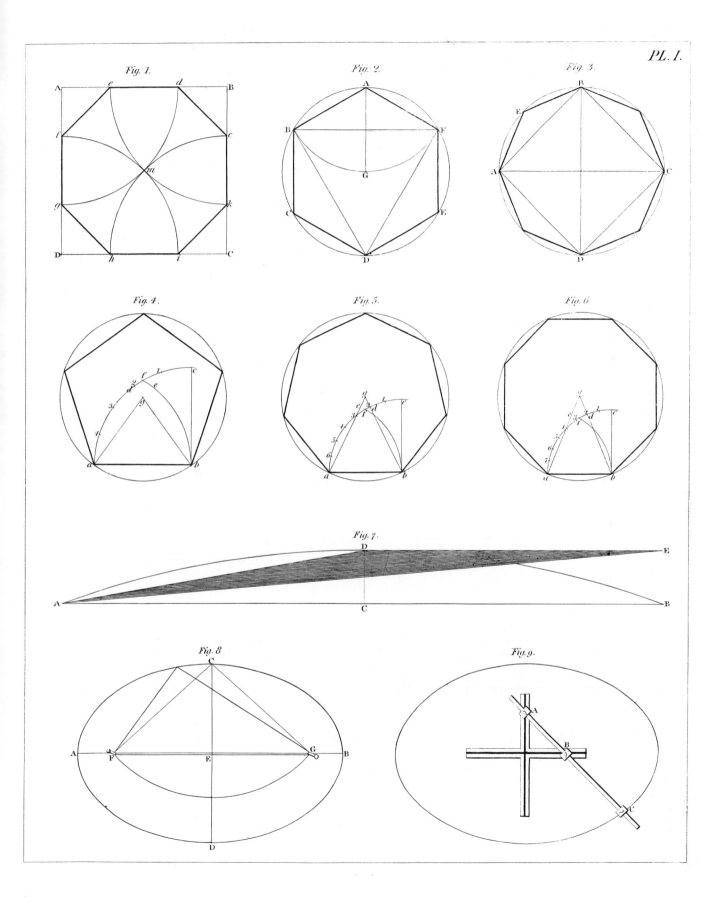

Fig. 1.

Fig. 2.

Fig. 3.

Fig. 4.

Fig. 5.

Fig. 6.

Fig. 7.

Fig. 8.

Fig. 9.

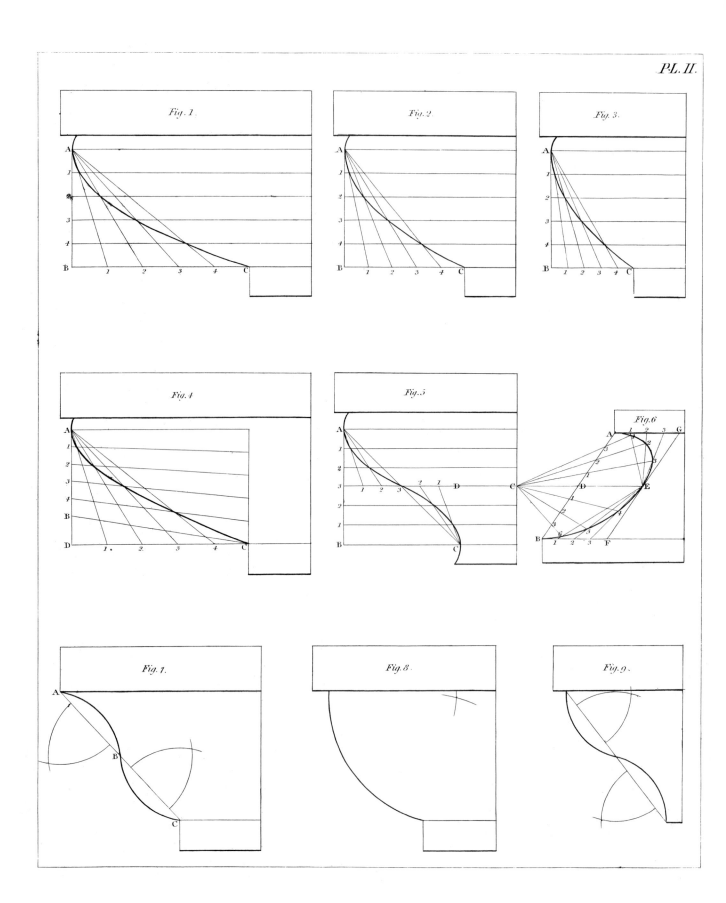

Fig. 1.

Fig. 2.

Fig. 3.

Fig. 4.

Fig. 5.

Fig. 6.

Fig. 7.

Fig. 8.

Fig. 9.

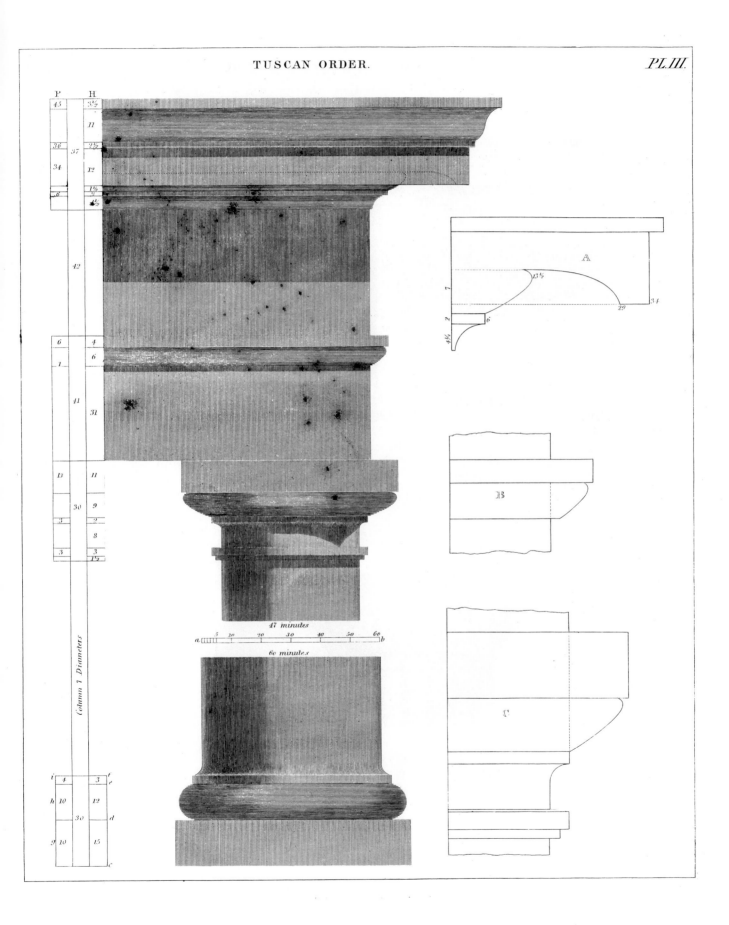

47 minutes

60 minutes

Column 7 Diameters

DORIC ORDER *From the Temple of Thesus at Athens* PL. IV.

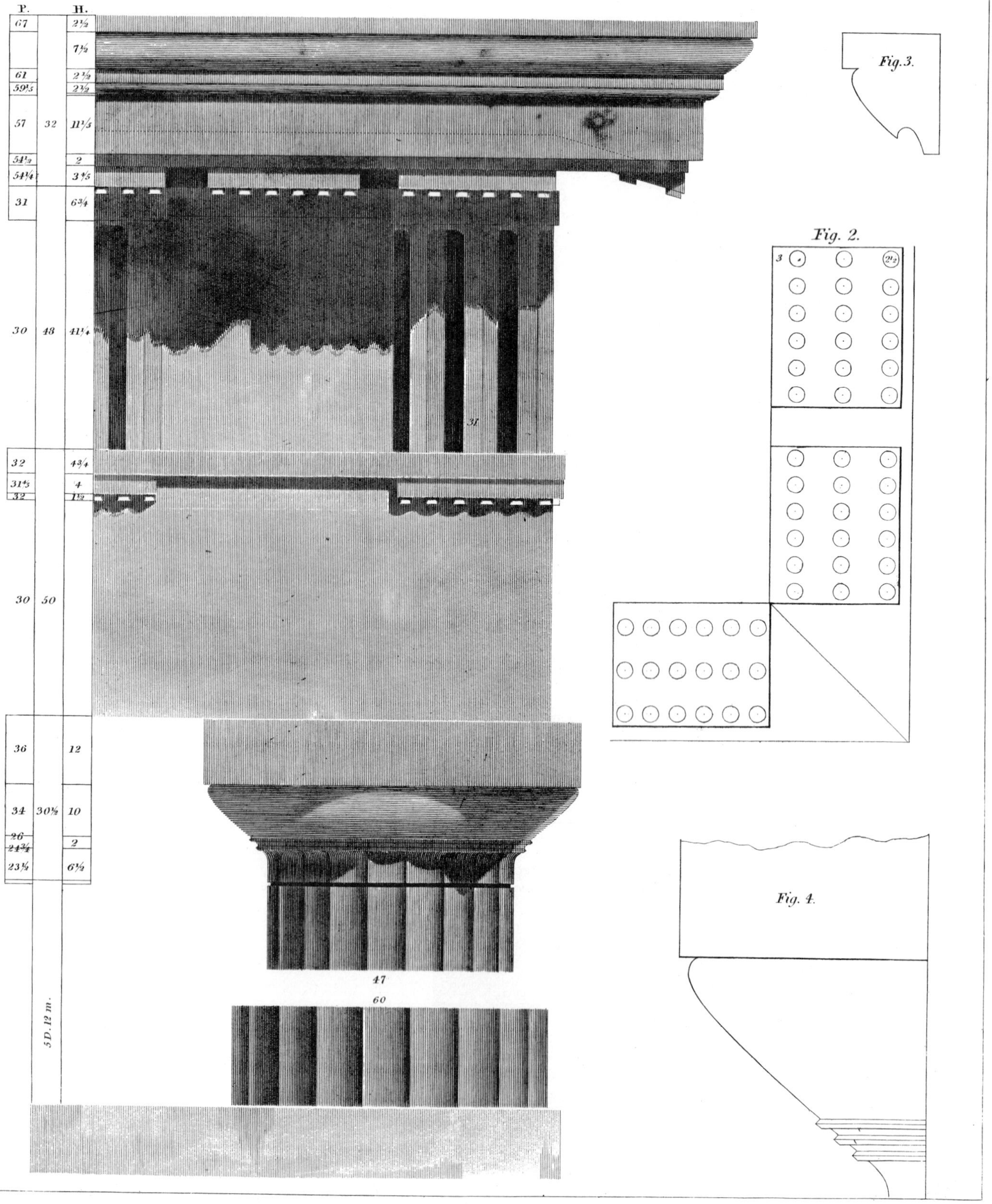
P.
H.
67
2½
7½
61
2½
59⅗
2½
57
32
11⅗
54½
2
54¼
3⅘
31
6¾
30
48
41¼
31
32
4¾
31⅘
4
32
1½
30
50
36
12
34
30½
10
26
24¾
2
23½
6½
47
60
5 D. 12 m.
Fig. 3.
Fig. 2.
3
2½
Fig. 4.

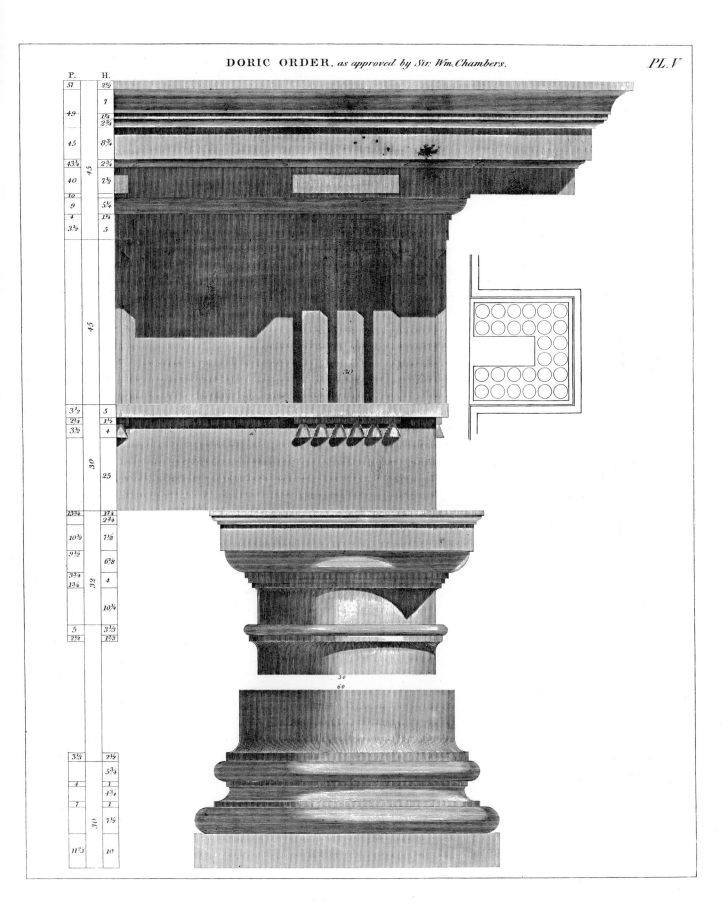

fore, it may be sixteen and a third, sixteen and a half, or sixteen and two thirds, modules high, in interior decorations even seventeen modules, and sometimes, perhaps, a trifle more; which increase in the height may be added entirely to the shaft, without changing either the base or capital. The entablature, too, may remain unaltered in all the aforesaid cases; for it will be sufficiently bold without alteration."—*Chambers on Civil Architecture.*

DORIC ORDER, EXAMPLE No. 3.

PLATE VI.

This example is compiled chiefly from the best Grecian specimens of the Doric order, with such alterations, as, it was thought, would render it more simple, less expensive, and better adapted to the materials of which it is usually composed in this country.

In the capital the annulets have been changed for those of the Roman character, because it is supposed that the annulets of the Grecian Doric are too small and indistinct to comport with the other members of that massive composition. Not that the Grecian annulets are not, of themselves, beautiful; but, their number being constantly from three to five, and the space they occupy not generally exceeding two minutes, when three, the smallest number, are used, it requires nine lines for angles to separate them from each other and the adjoining members, which lines, or angles, if equally divided, could not occupy a larger space than one fourth of a minute each. It is therefore evident that, when the column, which they adorn, is not of large dimensions, they must, from the smallness of their size, and the small space which they occupy, appear confused and indistinct.

In practice, I have sometimes retained the Grecian arrangement of the annulets, but reduced their number to two, and made them occupy a space of two and a half minutes. In imitation of the Roman and modern practice, the faces of the frize and architrave are both in the same plane. The face of the architrave, and those of the triglyphs, were likewise in the same plane in the best specimens of the Grecian Doric; but, in order to have these in the same plane, the frize must be recessed back the whole thickness of the triglyph—a practice which would be inconvenient for us, when the material is of wood, because a difficulty will then exist in preventing leakage between the frize and architrave; whereas, in the former practice, that difficulty was removed by the tenia covering and securing the joint between the frize and architrave.

The size and form of the drops below the triglyphs have been made to assume the Roman character, because those in the Grecian examples are supposed to be too small and indistinct. The mutules over the metopes have been left off in further imitation of the Romans; and, where simplicity only is desired, it is believed that object is obtained with one over each triglyph. As practice seems to require that some determinate height should be given to the column, in compliance thereto, I give it seven diameters including its capital. This is a lighter proportion than the Greek, but heavier than the Roman. The entablature is two diameters in height. The shaft of the column is decorated with twenty flutes without fillets, the sections of which, when made of wood, may be segments of circles, or nearly so, because, if made of a part of an ellipsis, as in the Greek original, there will not be sufficient strength in the wood to prevent the edges between the flutes from fracture; when the material is stone, or iron, they should invariably form a part of an ellipsis, as the effect produced thereby is more beautiful than that of the stiff, tasteless segment of a circle. The shaft of the column diminishes thirteen minutes, and the line of its sides may be straight, or, which is preferable, slightly curved, the convex side of the curve turning outward. The triglyphs in the frize are thirty minutes in front, and their distance from each other, reckoning from the centre of each, is seventy-five minutes.

Fig. 1 represents a drop of the mutule, the corona, cimatium and the ovolo.

Fig. 2 represents the capital on a large scale, figured in minutes.

The curves of these mouldings have been carefully drawn, and it is believed that they will appear very graceful, if correctly imitated.

A, on fig. 2, shows that the face of the architrave is in a vertical line with the upper fillet of the capital, which projects three and a half minutes from the neck of the column.

In the Roman and modern examples, a difficulty exists, where columns and undiminished pilasters were employed in supporting the same entablature, because there is given to the pilasters the same diameter as to the column, and the lower fascia of the architrave is situated in a vertical line with the neck of the column. It therefore happens that the neck of the pilaster projects beyond the face of the architrave; which defect they endeavor to avoid by diminishing the pilaster. But pilasters of the same diameter with the columns have the appearance of being larger than the columns, on account of their form being angular, and that of the column round; and a pilaster certainly is larger, viewed from any other situation than directly in front.

I have, in this example, endeavored to avoid both defects, by making the diameter of the pilaster equal to that of the upper fillet of the capital, which, in this order, is fifty-four minutes; so that the lower fascia of the architrave is in a vertical line with the neck of the pilaster. What is here said with regard to the diameter of pilasters will apply to both the Tuscan and Ionic orders.

It will be observed, by reading the description of pediments, that the Grecians never employed either mutules, dentils or modillions in the cornices of the sloping sides of their pediments. I have therefore, on plate 34, fig. 1, given an example of a cornice suitably constructed for that purpose, which is figured in minutes.

RAKING MOULDINGS.

PLATE VII.

FIG. 1.

Let A be the given moulding, B the raking moulding, and C the return moulding. Draw a 9 in A, a 9 in B, and a 9 in C; make a 9 in B at right angles with the rake of the pediment, and a 9 in C and A both perpendicular. Take the projection 8 9 in A, and set it from 9 to 8 on both B and C; draw a 8 in A B and C; divide the given moulding A into eight parts, and draw lines through each of these parts parallel to the rake of the pediment; then take the distance 1 1 from the given moulding, A, and prick it down from 1 to 1 on the line a 8 in both B and C, and take the distance 2 2, 3 3, 5 5, 6 6, and 7 7, and set them down on the line a 8 in B and C, as before directed; then, through the parts so set off, trace the curve, which will be the outline of the raking and the return moulding.

At fig. 3 is shown a design for a triglyph, including the fillet and drops below it, drawn on a large scale; the sides of a drop would meet in a point if produced to e. Fig. 4 is a section which is taken from c to f. On fig. 3, and on fig. 2 at **A B**, is shown a section of the triglyph and its capital, also the under side of the ovolo and its fillet, showing the method of capping the triglyph, and disposing the fillet over the metopes. And on fig. 4 is shown the size and shape of the lower end of the drops; the dotted line shows the size and shape of the top end where they join the fillet above it. The different members are figured in minutes on the plate.

BASE MOULDINGS.

PLATE VIII.

A REPRESENTS the soffit of the Doric cornice to example No. 3.
B is a design for a Doric base by **St. Le Clerc.**
C is a design for an Ionic base by **Vignola;** and
D is a design of the Corinthian base, taken from the portico of the Rotunda at Rome.

GRECIAN IONIC ORDER.

PLATE IX.

IN Ionia, the temple of Apollo Panionius was built after the **Doric** manner; but that refined people, not satisfied with the simplicity of this order, invented another of a more delicate character, and named it after their own country, the Ionic. They made the height of the column greater in proportion to its diameter than in the Doric; the capital was totally different in principle, the entablature was changed in its members and proportions, and a base was added to the bottom of the column. Vitruvius says that, as the Doric was strong and masculine, the Ionians modelled their order with female delicacy, and that the volutes were taken from the curls of hair on each side of the face.

In the architrave and frieze, all appearances of triglyphs and guttæ are omitted; and in the cornice, instead of the bold mutules of the Doric, the ends of smaller pieces of wood, to which the covering tiles were fixed, are represented by what are termed dentils or teeth. This order differed from the Doric, by having a base at the lower extremity of the shaft; the propriety of this might have arisen from the diameter of the shaft being much less than that of the Doric, in proportion to the height of the order, or the weight it had to sustain.

The volute is the great distinguishing feature of this order. In the Athenian Ionics, and in the temple of Minerva Polias at Priene, the lower edge of the channel which runs between them is formed into a curve, bending downwards in the middle, and revolving about the spirals on either side. In the temple of Erectheus and Minerva Polias at Athens, each volute has two channels, formed by two distinct spiral borders; the borders forming the exterior volute, and the under side of the lower channel, have between them a deep recess or spiral groove, which diminishes gradually in breadth, till it loses itself in the centre of the eye. In the temple of Bacchus at Teos, the great theatre of Laodicea, and in all the Roman Ionics, the channel whereby the two volutes are connected has no border on the lower edge, but terminates with a horizontal line, falling in a tangent to the commencement of the second revolution of each volute.

The capitals of both Greek and Roman Ionics have the echinus, astragal, and fillet; the echinus is always cut into eggs, surrounded with borders of angular sections, with tongues between them; the astragal consists of a row of beads, having two small ones inserted between two large ones. In all the Roman buildings, except the Coliseum, these mouldings are cut in the same manner. The height of the Ionic column was originally eight diameters; the moderns have increased it to nine. The shaft is generally cut into twenty-four flutes, with as many fillets.

The section of the flutes of the columns, in the temple on the Illyssus at Athens, is elliptical; the flutes descend and follow the curve of the scape of the column in the following specimens, viz.: the temple of Minerva Polias and of Erectheus at Athens; the temple of Bacchus at Teos; and Minerva Polias at Priene.

The base of the Athenian Ionics consists of two tori, having a scotia between them, separated from the tori, above and below, by two fillets; the fillet above the inferior torus projects, in general, as far as the extremity of the superior torus, and the fillet beneath the upper torus projects beyond both. The scotia is very flat, its section forming an elliptic curve, which joins the fillet on either side. The tori and scotia are nearly of equal altitudes. In the temple on the Illyssus, there is a bead and fillet on the upper torus, joining the fillet to the scape of the column; the upper torus of the base is fluted; but the lower part, which joins the upper surface of the fillet above the scotia, is left entire.

On account of the frieze being wanting in most of the Asiatic remains, although the architrave and cornice have been accurately measured, the height of the entablature cannot be ascertained. The only instance in which a frieze has been discovered is in the theatre of Laodicea; and there it is rather less than one fifth of the entablature. The height of the entablature may, in general, be two diameters; and it may be increased in works of magnificence.

In the temple of Erectheus and Minerva Polias at Athens, the architrave has three fasciæ and a cymatium. In the temple of Bacchus at Teos, and Minerva Polias at Priene, the architraves are also divided into three fasciæ below the cymatium. Their proportions are very different from those at Athens, though also elegant in character and effect.

In all the Asiatic Ionics, the crowning mouldings of the cornices are cimarecta, less in projection than in height. The dentil bands are never omitted. The cymatium of the denticulated band is recessed upwards, being almost entirely wrought out of the soffit of the corona, which nearly conceals its height.

When Ionic columns stand in the flanks as well as in the fronts of buildings, two volutes at the corner of each angular column are contrived so as to present the same form in the flank as in the front, as in the temple of Bacchus at Teos; of Minerva at Priene; Erectheus, and that of the muses at Athens; and likewise of Fortuna Virilis at Rome: the angular capitals have, in all these instances, one volute on each side, projected in a curve towards the angle. Amongst the ancient Romans, as at the temple of Concord at Rome, the capitals of all the columns are made to face the four sides of the abacus; and it was from this specimen that Scammozzi, encouraged by the example of Michael Angelo, composed the capital upon this principle, which bears his name.

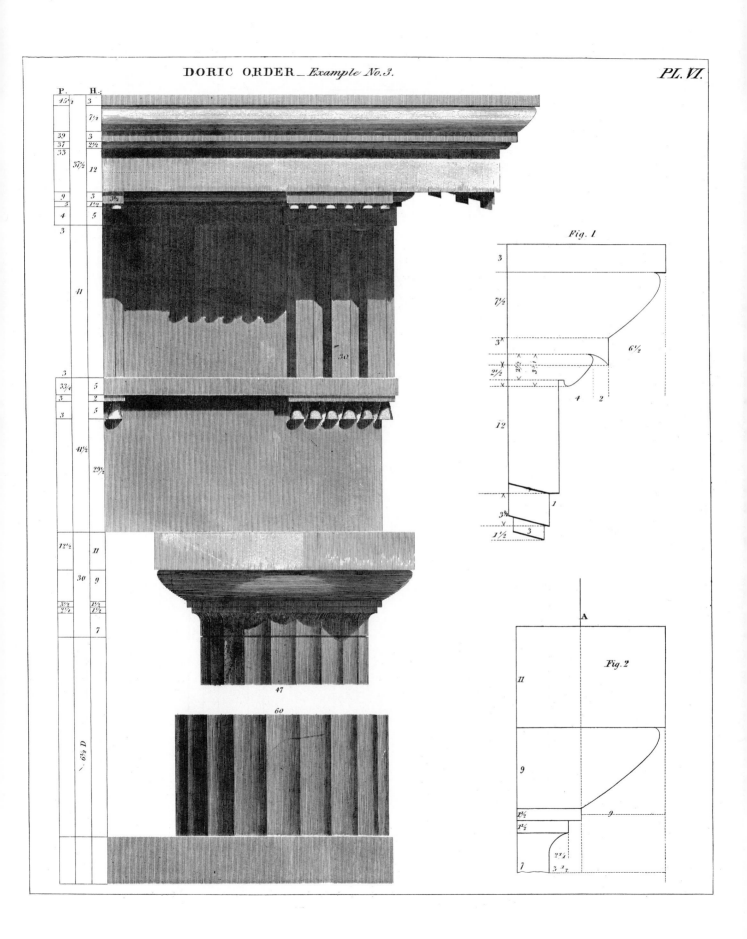

Fig. 1

Fig. 2

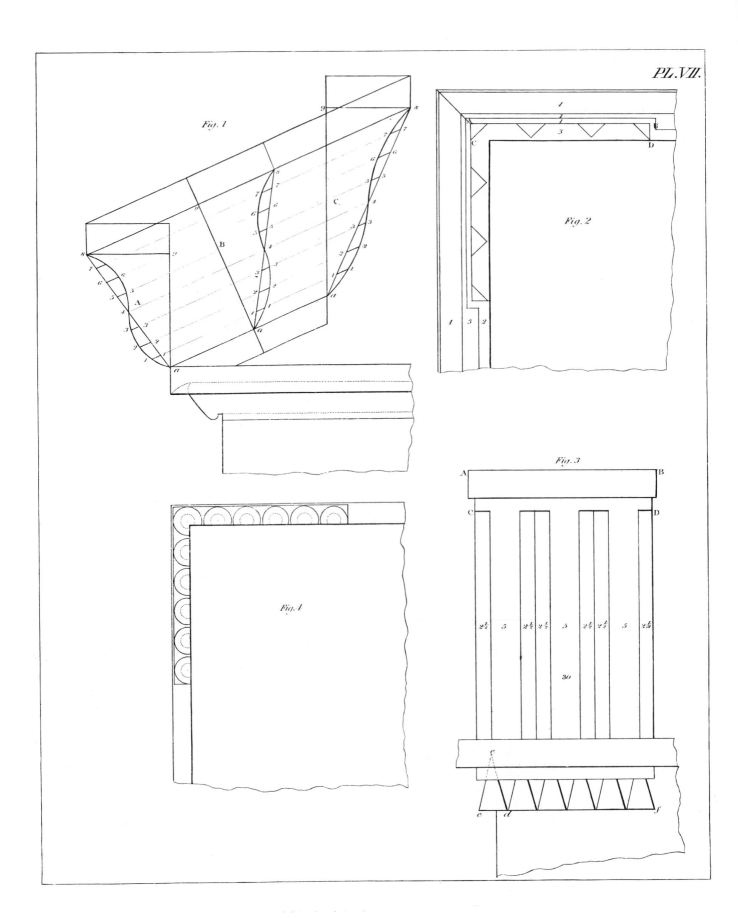

Fig. 1

Fig. 2

Fig. 3

Fig. 4

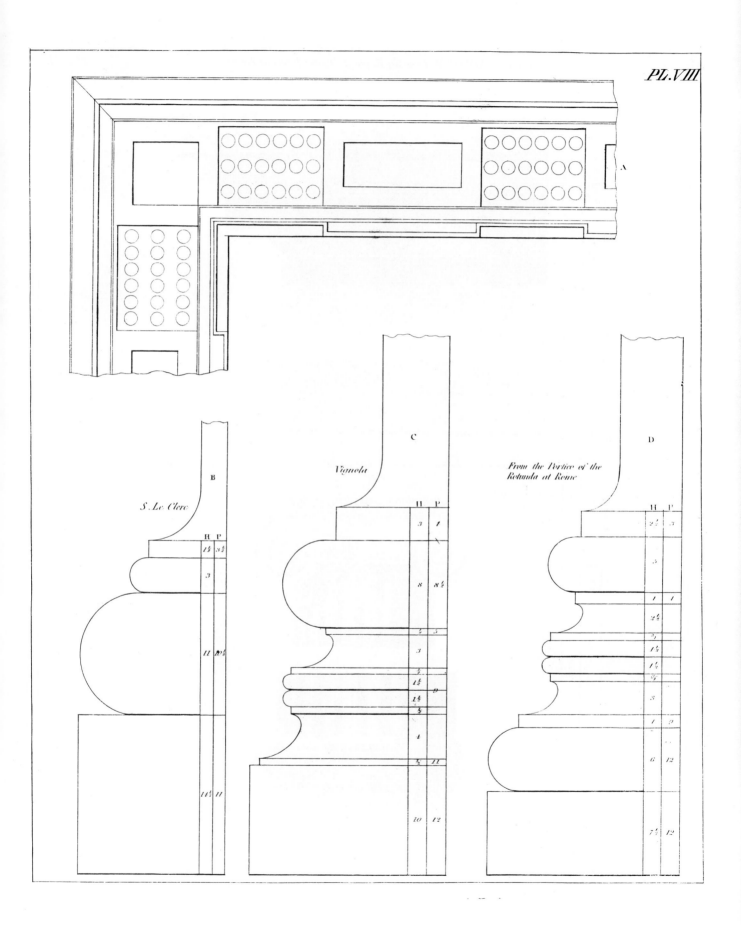

PL.VIII

A

B

S. Le Clerc

H P
1½ 3½
3

11 10½

10½ 11

C

Vignola

H P
3   1

8   8½

5   5
3
½
1½ 9
1½
½
1
4

½   11

10   12

D

From the Portico of the
Rotunda at Rome

H P
2½ 3

5

1   1
2½
3½
1½
1½
3½
3

1   9

6   12

7½ 12

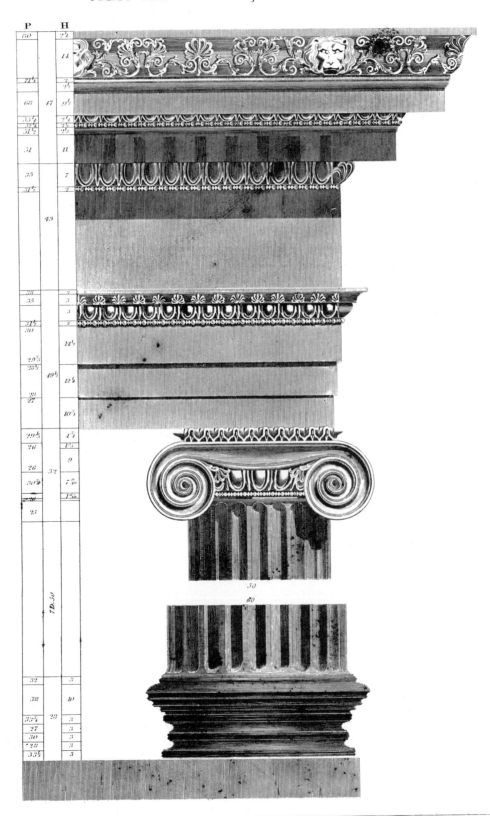

Fig. 3

Fig. 1

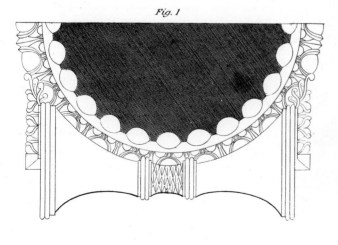

Fig. 2

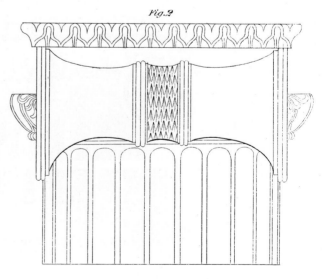

Side of Capital.

Profile of Capital.

Plan of Capital.

Elevation of the Ionic Order on the Temple of Minerva Polias at Priene.

The great height of the cimarecta and its small projection is of itself beautiful, and well calculated for ornament.

The dentils show to great advantage, their bold projections making them a striking feature in this order.

The architrave and capital are well proportioned and elegant; and the surprising delicacy of the ornaments, their bold relief, and the grand ratio of the parts to each other, render this example one of the most beautiful of the Ionic order.

GRECIAN IONIC CAPITAL.

PLATE X.

Fig. 1 represents one half the plan of an Ionic capital; fig. 2, a side; and fig. 3, a front elevation of the same capital on a large scale.

ROMAN IONIC ORDER.

PLATE XI.

Ionic Order, as approved by Sir William Chambers.

"Amongst the ancients, the form of the Ionic profile appears to have been more positively determined than that of any other order;

for in all the antiques at Rome, the temple of Concord excepted, it is exactly the same, and conformable to the description Vitruvius has given thereof.

"The modern artists have likewise been more unanimous in their opinions upon the subject; all of them, excepting Palladio and his imitators, having employed the dentil cornice, and the other parts of the profile, nearly as they are found in the Coliseum, the temple of Fortune, and the theatre of Marcellus.

"In this plate of the Ionic order, there is a design of the antique profile, collected by me from different antiquities of Rome. The height of the column is eighteen modules, and that of the entablature four modules and a half, or quarter of the height of the column, as in the other orders; which is a trifle less than in any of the regular antique Ionics. The base is Attic, as in all the antiques, and the shaft of the column may either be plain or fluted, with twenty-four or with twenty flutings only, as at the temple of Fortune; of which the plan should be a little more than semicircular, as it is at the temple of Jupiter Tonans, and at the forum of Nerva; because then they are more distinctly marked. The fillet, or interval between the flutes, should not be broader than one third of their width, nor narrower than one quarter thereof. The ornaments of the capital are to correspond with the flutes of the shaft; and there must be an ove or a dart above the middle of each flute.

" Vignola and Scammozzi, Serlio, Alberti, and others, have, in their architraves, imitated those of the theatre of Marcellus, and of the Coliseum, having composed them of three fasciæ, distinguished from each other only by small projections. This has but an indifferent effect; the separations so faintly marked are not sufficiently striking, and the architrave is left too destitute of ornaments for the rest of the profile—a defect most striking whenever the mouldings of the profile are enriched.

"On the other hand, Palladio's and De L'Orme's architraves appear too rich, being likewise composed of three fasciæ, separated by mouldings; I have therefore, in this particular, chosen to imitate the profile of the temple of Antoninus and Faustina, where there are only two fasciæ, separated from each other by a moulding.

"The three parts of the entablature bear the same proportion to each other in this as in the Tuscan order; the frieze is plain, as being most suitable to the simplicity of the rest of the composition, and the cornice is almost an exact copy from Vignola's design, in which there is a purity of form, a grandeur of style, and a close conformity to the most approved antiques, not to be found in the profiles of his competitors.

"If it be required to reduce this entablature to two ninths of the height of the column, which, on most occasions, is a proportion preferable to that of one quarter, particularly where the eye has been habituated to contemplate diminutive objects, it may easily be done by making the module for the entablature less by one ninth than the semi-diameter of the column; afterwards dividing it as usual, and observing the same dimensions as are figured in the design. The distribution of the dentil band will, in such case, answer pretty nearly in all the regular intercolumniations; and in the outer angle there will be a dentil, as in the temple of Fortune at Rome.

"In interior decorations, where much delicacy is required, the height of the entablature may be reduced even to one fifth of the column, by observing the same method, and making the module only four fifths of the semi-diameter.

" The antique Ionic capital differs from any of the others : its front and side faces are not alike. This particularity occasions great difficulty, wherever there are breaks in the entablature, or where the decoration is continued in flank, as well as in front; for either all the capitals in front must have the baluster side outward, or the angular capitals will have a different appearance from the rest; neither of which is admissible. The architect of the temple of Fortune at Rome has fallen upon an expedient, which, in some degree, remedies the defect. In that building, the corner capitals have their angular volutes in an oblique position, inclining equally to the front and side, and offering volute faces both ways.

"In this order, I have employed the Attic base. Of the antique base, described by Vitruvius, and used by Vignola and Philibert De L'Orme in their Ionic orders, and by Sir Christopher Wren in some parts of St. Paul's, I think there is no example among the antiques; and, being universally esteemed a very imperfect production, I have not even given a design of it.

"As the Doric order is particularly affected in churches or temples dedicated to male saints, so the Ionic is principally used in such as are consecrated to females of the matronal state. It is likewise employed in courts of justice, in libraries, colleges, seminaries, and other structures having relation to arts or letters; in private houses and palaces, to adorn the women's apartments; and, says Le Clerc, in all places dedicated to peace and tranquillity. The ancients employed it in temples sacred to Juno, to Bacchus, to Diana, and other deities whose dispositions held a medium between the severe and the effeminate."—*Chambers on Civil Architecture.*

IONIC ORDER, EXAMPLE No. 3.

PLATE XII.

In selecting the following example, regard has been had for the materials of which it is usually wrought, for economy, and for its adaptation to present practice. In imitation of Palladio and other modern architects, the column is nine diameters in height; the shaft is decorated with twenty-four flutes, and as many fillets; the base is Attic, as with the Romans in their best examples, and is decidedly preferable to those employed by the Greeks in their early practice of this order. The capital is taken from a beautiful capital found at the little Ionic temple near the river Illyssus at Athens, which is a fine example for our imitation. To the height of the entablature two diameters of the column have been given. The architrave is thirty-seven and a half minutes in height, and is divided into two fascies, separated by a rectangular projection, and capped by the echinus, which is finished by a fillet above and below it. The frieze is plain, and thirty-six minutes in height. The cornice is forty-six and a half minutes in height, the bed-mould of which is enriched with the dentil, its legitimate ornament, finished with the echinus and bead below, and above with the echinus and fillet, both of which are recessed up into the soffit of the corona, so as to be concealed from a direct front view. The corona is eleven minutes in height, and is capped by a compound moulding, which pretty nearly imitates the Grecian specimens.

Fig. 1 is a section of the cymatium, showing the fascia and cima-recta on a large scale.

Fig. 2 is a design of the ovolo and fillet above the dentil, completely recessed up into the soffit of the corona.

Fig. 3 shows a profile of the mouldings of the capital on a large scale.

GRECIAN ENTABLATURES.

PLATE XIII.

ON this plate are exhibited two ancient examples of entablatures. That of fig. 1 is imitated from the little Ionic temple near the river Illyssus at Athens. It is two diameters and seventeen minutes in height, and is remarkable for its simple plainness. Its details, beautiful in themselves, are judiciously arranged, and appear dignified and chaste. The dentil, however, which, it must be allowed, is the legitimate and characteristic ornament of the Ionic order, is here omitted. It will be wise, nevertheless, to imitate this example when simple dignity only is required, because a very considerable portion of labour in its execution will thereby be saved, which would be required to execute an entablature more abundant in mouldings, and in which the dentil should form a part of the bed-mould, especially if the material be stone.

Fig. 2 exhibits a capital and entablature imitated from the Choragic monuments of Thrasyllus at Athens. Although this example is neither Doric, Ionic, nor Corinthian, it is beautiful in both character and effect. It is believed, however, that a deviation from the original in some of its details will render it more conformable to modern practice than it would otherwise be. It is with great deference to its ancient author, that the following deviations are proposed;—first, to leave off the cimatium, which crowns the capital, because the capital is too abundant in mouldings; second, to leave off the drops or guttæ, which are suspended from the fillet of the regula, because they are so small, and, when placed in a row, produce the idea of finery rather than of dignity to the composition; and, lastly, to give a greater projection to the bed-mould, and a less height to the fillet by which it is crowned.

PLATE XIV.

On Plate **XIV.** are two designs for entablatures. **Fig. 2** has the **D**oric proportions, and is intended to be used with plain columns or pilasters of that order, without a base, and where plainness only is desired, or expense is to be avoided. The capital accompanying this entablature is intended to be used with pilasters only, and was designed as a substitute for that beautiful but complicated one belonging to the Choragic monument of Thrasyllus, at Athens. The great number and delicacy of the parts of this capital render it expensive, and very difficult to be worked, even in wood; and it is almost impossible to work it in granite.

The one on this plate, intended for a substitute, is composed of few and large parts, and is of such a construction as to be easily worked on either wood or granite.

Fig. **1** is intended to be used with **I**onic columns, or pilasters, where simplicity of character is desired. Fig. 3 shows the band of the architrave on a large scale; and fig. 4 shows the crown moulding, also on a large scale.

PLATE XV.

On Plate **XV.** is a design for an Ionic entablature with modillions.

The modillion does not properly belong to the Ionic cornice, but, as it has been so frequently used by Palladio and other modern architects, I thought it best to give a design of one here, for fear that, otherwise, I might disappoint some, who rigidly adhere to the Roman school of architecture. It will be seen by the plate, that the capping of the modillion is a square instead of an ogee, and that it is recessed up into the soffit of the corona, and by that means forms a pannel between the modillions.

Fig. **1.** To draw the soffit of the modillion, divide the line *a b* into six equal parts; on **2**, with the distance **1 2**, draw *g h;* on *e*, with the distance two and one half parts, draw *h i :* and with the same distance, and on *d*, draw *i b*.

Fig. 2 is a design for a cornice. See explanation of Plates **XXXIV.** and **XXXV.**

VOLUTES.

PLATE XVI.

To draw the Ionic Volute.

FIG. 1.

THE centre of the eye **N** and the distance **A** being given, on the centre **N**, and with a radius equal to one half the diameter of the eye, describe a circle, cutting **N A** at **O**; divide **O A** into two equal parts at **E**, and divide **O E** into one part more than you intend to have revolutions in the volute; then take one of those divisions for

Fig. 1.

Fig. 2.

Fig. 3.

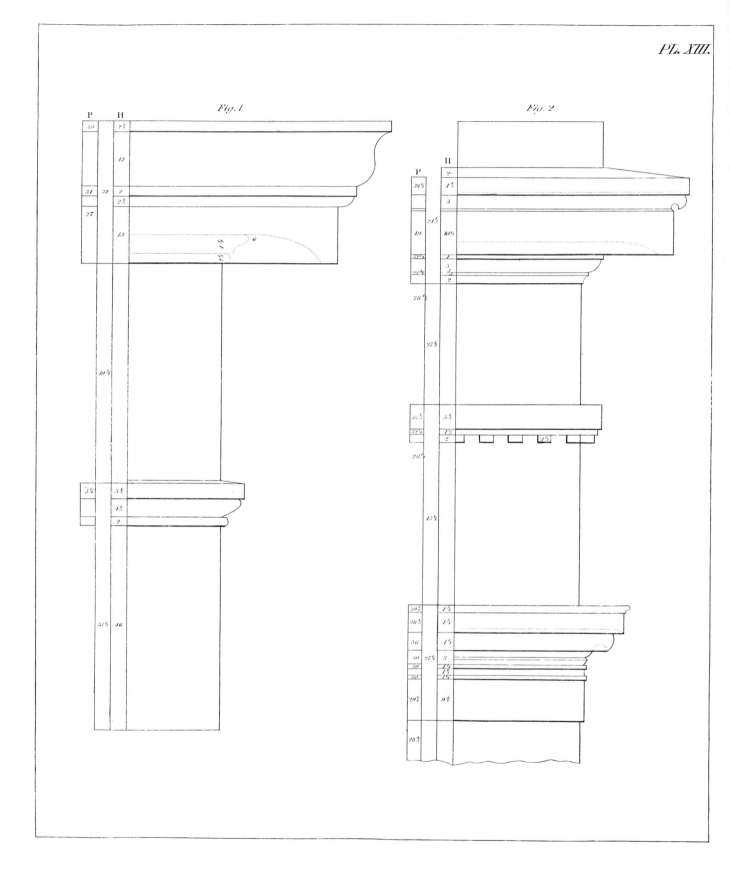

Fig. 1

Fig. 2

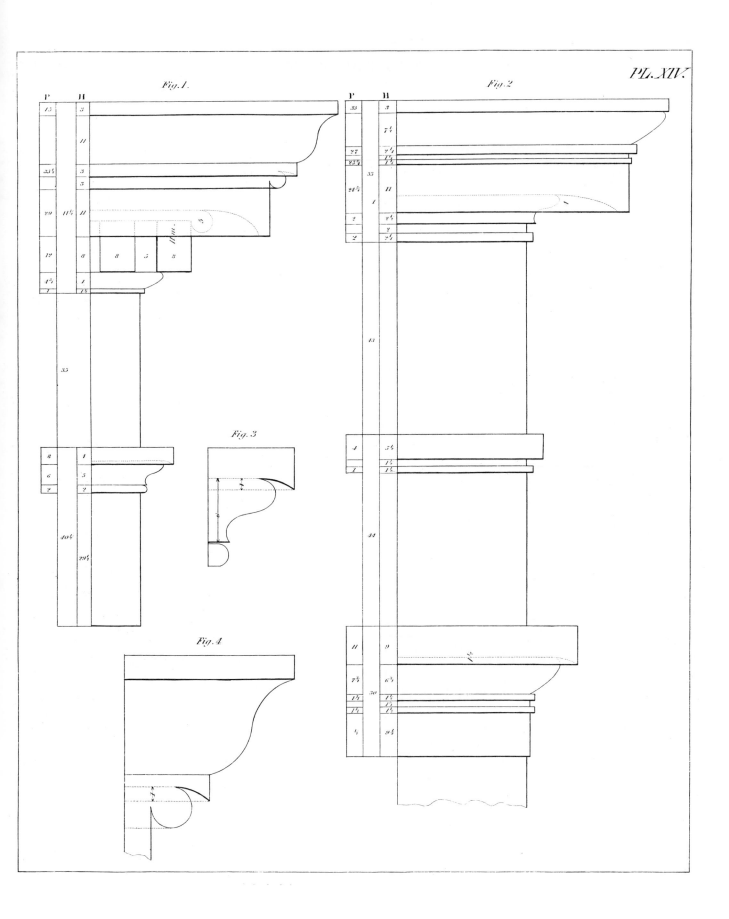

Fig.1.

Fig.2.

Fig.3.

Fig.4.

IONIC ENTABLATURE

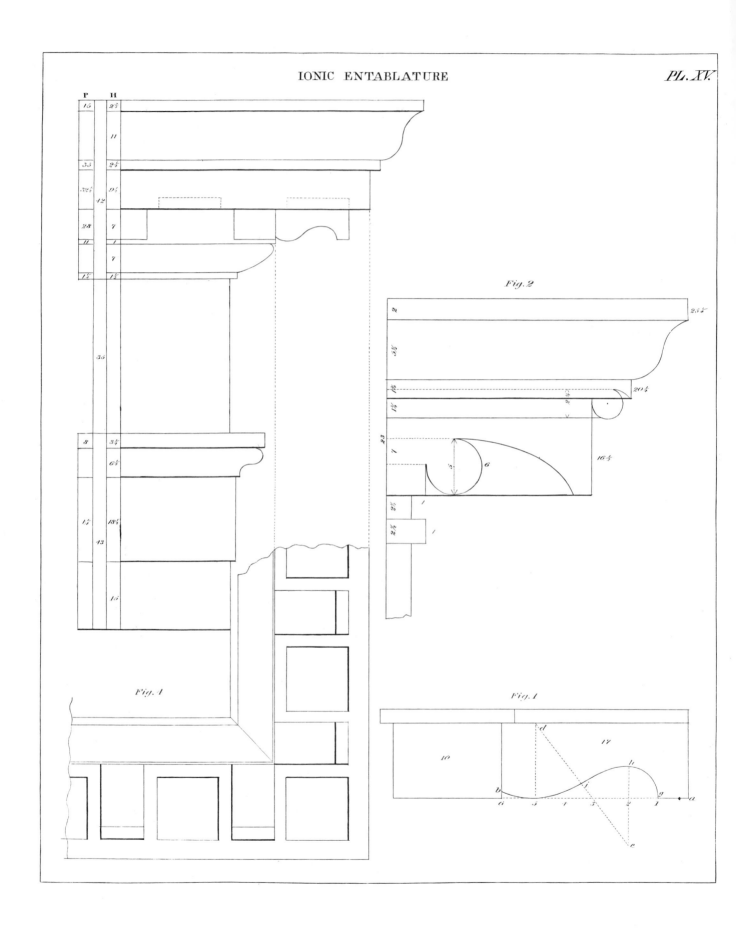

PL. XV.

Fig. 2

Fig. 1

Fig. 1

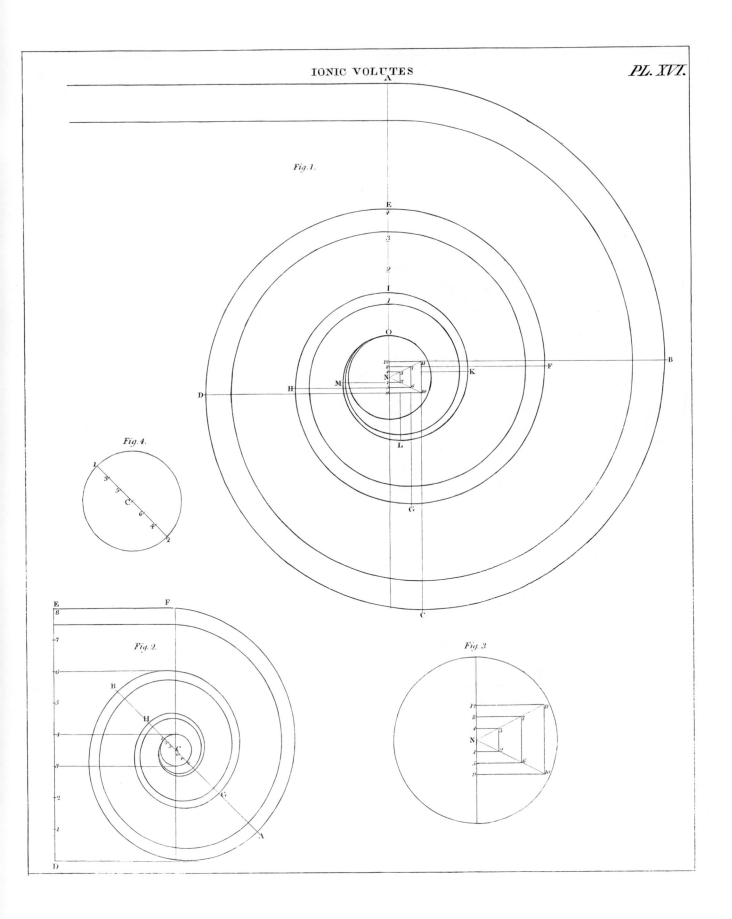

Fig.1.

Fig.4.

Fig.2.

Fig.3.

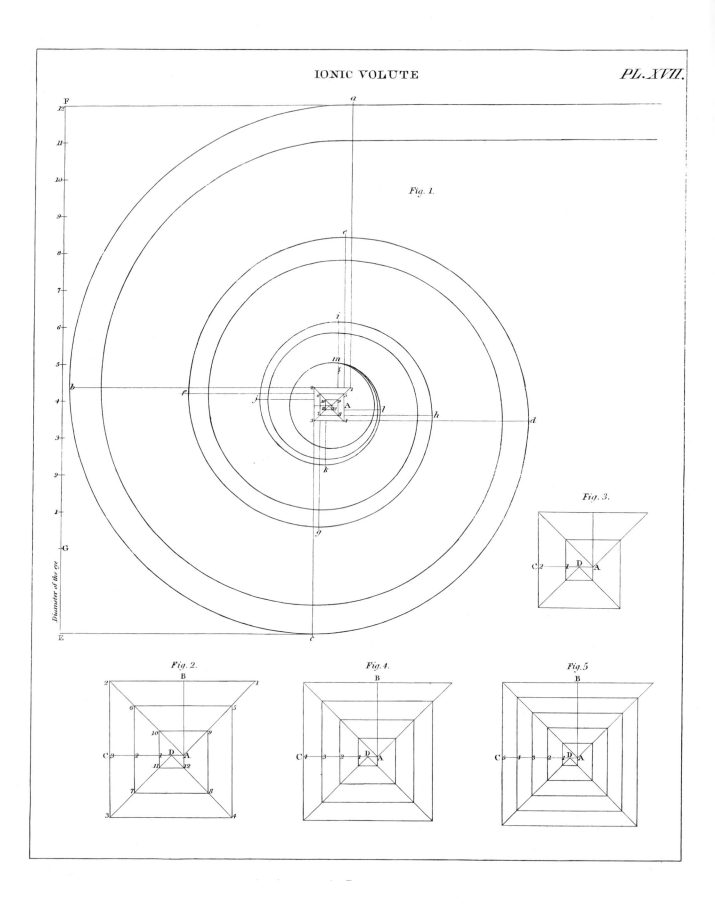

Fig. 1.

Fig. 2.

Fig. 3.

Fig. 4.

Fig. 5.

Diameter of the eye

the side of the square **9, 10, 11** and **12**, and divide it as is shown on a larger scale at fig. 3; then, with the distance **12 A** in your compasses, and on **12**, draw the quarter of a circle **A B**. Then on **11**, and with the distance **11 B**, draw the quarter circle **B C**; on **10**, and with the distance **10 C**, draw **C D**; on **9**, with the distance **9 D**, draw **D E**. This completes one revolution. On **8** draw **E F**; on **7** draw **F G**; on **6** draw **G H**; on **5** draw **H I**; on **4** draw **I K**; on **3** draw **K L**; on **2** draw **L M**; and on **1** draw **M O**; which completes the outside circle. Draw the inside circle, from centres one fifth part of one of the divisions of the square nearer the centre of the eye of the volute.

FIG. 2.

The height of the volute **D E** being given, divide it into eight equal parts; take one of those parts for the diameter of the eye, leaving four parts above and three below the eye; then draw the diagonal line **A B**, cutting the centre of the eye at **C**, and divide **1 2** into six equal parts, as is more clearly seen on the eye at large, fig. 4. With the radius **1 F**, and on **1**, draw the arc **F A**; on **2**, and with the distance **2 A**, draw **A B**; on **3**, with the distance **3 B**, draw **B G**; and so on, until you have completed the outside of the fillet; draw the inside of the fillet from centres one fifth part of one division nearer the centre, as before directed.

PLATE XVII.

To draw a Spiral Line to touch a given Circle, whose Centre is the Centre of the Spiral, to any Number of Revolutions; the whole Height being given.

From the height of the spiral **F E**, set off the diameter of the eye **E G**. If three revolutions are intended, divide **G F** into twelve equal parts: if four revolutions, divide **G F** into sixteen equal parts. Take seven of the twelve parts, together with one half of the eye or one half of **E G**, and set it from **F** downwards, and it will extend to the centre of the eye, **A**. In fig. 2 the centres are drawn on a large scale, from which I shall make the description; which will also make plain fig. 3, which is calculated for two, fig. 4, which is calculated for four, and fig. 5, which is calculated for five revolutions.

A is the centre of the eye just found; make **A B** perpendicular to **A C**, and each equal to one half of one of the twelve parts of **G F**. Fig. 1. Make **B 1, B 2** and **C 2** each equal to **A B** or **A C**; draw **A 1** and **A 2**; divide **A C** into 3 equal parts, or into as many parts as it is intended to make revolutions in the volute: divide **A 1** on **A C** into two parts at **D**; draw **D 4** parallel to **A 2**, **D 3** parallel to **A 1**: then draw lines cutting the diagonals at **3, 4, 5, 6, 7, 8, 9, 10, 11** and **12**, which will be the twelve centres, from which the volute is to be drawn. In fig. 1, and on **1** as a centre, with the distance **1 a**, draw the quadrant of a circle *a b;* on **2**, with the distance **2 b**, draw *b c;* on **3** draw *c d;* on **4** draw *d e;* on **5** draw *e f;* on **6** draw *f g;* on **7** draw *g h;* on **8** draw *h i;* on **9** draw *i j;* on **10** draw *j k;* on **11** draw *k l;* and on **12** draw *l m;* and the outside of the fillet is completed. Draw the inside line, as before directed.

CORINTHIAN ORDER.

PLATE XVIII.

THE artists of Græcia proper, perceiving that, in the Ionic order, the severity of the Doric had been departed from, by one happy effort, invented a third, which still much surpassed the Ionic in delicacy of proportion and richness of decorations : this was named the Corinthian order. The merit of this invention is ascribed to Callimachus, an Athenian sculptor, who is said to have had the idea suggested to him, by observing acanthus leaves growing around a basket which had been placed, with some favorite trinkets, upon the grave of a young lady of Corinth ; the stalks which arose among the leaves having been formed into slender volutes by a square tile, which covered the basket. The whole fabric of the Corinthian order is composed with great delicacy of taste. It is admirably fitted for the most highly ornamented states of architecture, and is strongly expressive of the refinement and excellence to which the Greeks had carried their taste and skill in architecture and sculpture.

The Greeks, having invented and established three orders, with each a separate character, calculated for edifices, gradually ascending from the most simple to those which were highly ornamented, completed a distinct and perfect school of architecture, to which there remained nothing to be added.

In all the examples in Stuart's Athens, this order has an Attic base : the upper fillet of the scotia projects as far as the upper torus. In the monument of Lysicrates, the upper fillet of the base projects farther than the upper torus, which is an inverted ovolo.

Vitruvius observes, that the shaft of the column has the same proportions as the Ionic, except the difference which arose from the greater height of the capital, it being a whole diameter ; whereas the Ionic is only two thirds of it. But this column, including the base and capital, has by the moderns been increased to ten diameters in height. If the entablature is enriched, the shaft should be fluted : the number of flutes and fillets are generally twenty-four ; and frequently the lower third of the height has cables, or reeds, husks, spirally twisted ribands, or some sort of flowers inserted on them. The great distinguishing feature of this order is its capital, which has for two thousand years been acknowledged the greatest ornament of this school of architecture. The height is one diameter of the column; to which the moderns have added one sixth more.

The best specimens are, the monument of Lysicrates, the Stoa, and arch of Adrian, at Athens; and the Pantheon of Agrippa, and the three columns of the Campo Vaccino, at Rome.

This order seems never to have been much employed in Greece before the time of the Roman conquest; but this powerful people employed it almost exclusively in every part of their extensive empire; and it is accordingly in edifices constructed under their influence that the most perfect specimens are to be found. Vitruvius says, that Corinthian columns were sometimes surmounted by a Doric entablature; which is not supported by any antique example now to be found. His observation respecting the Ionic entablature over the same kind of columns is verified in a number of instances.

The arch of Adrian, at Athens, has a cornice with dentils, a plain frieze, an architrave with two plain fasciæ, and an Attic base.

A temple at Jackly, near Mylassa, has a cornice with dentils, a swelled frieze, an architrave with three plain fasciæ, and an Attic base.

At Salonica (the ancient Thessalonica) a building called the Incantada has a cornice with dentils, a swelled frieze ornamented with flutings, an architrave with three plain fasciæ, and an Attic base.

The temple of Vesta, or Tivoli, has a plain cornice, with the dentil band uncut, an ornamented frieze, an architrave with two fasciæ, divided by an astragal, and an Attic base.

The portico of Septimius Severus, in the same city, has a plain cornice, with a small uncut dentil band, a plain frieze, and an architrave with three fasciæ, divided by mouldings.

In all these instances, the entablature and base are similar to those generally observed in the Ionic order, from which these Corinthian examples differ only in the form of their capitals. But it will appear that the Romans attempted to give the Corinthian order a more distinct character, by appropriating to it a peculiar entablature and base, and thus making a complete order of what might be previously regarded as a composition ; in which light Vitruvius seems to have considered it.

The portico of the Pantheon has a cornice with modillions, and an uncut dentil band, a plain frieze, an architrave with two fasciæ, divided by mouldings, and a Corinthian base.

The temple of Peace, at Rome, has a cornice with modillions and dentils, a plain frieze, and an architrave with three fasciæ, divided by mouldings.

In the Campo Vaccino, the three columns, supposed by some to have belonged to a temple of Jupiter Stator, and by others, to a temple dedicated to Julius Cæsar, have a cornice with modillions and dentils, a flat frieze, an architrave with three fasciæ, divided by mouldings, and a Corinthian base.

The temple of Jupiter Tonans, at Rome, has a cornice with modillions and dentils, a flat frieze, and an architrave with three fasciæ, divided by mouldings. The arch of Constantine has a cornice with modillions and dentils, a plain frieze, an architrave with three plain fasciæ, and an Attic base.

At Ephesus, the temple supposed by Chandler to have been erected by permission of Augustus, in honor of his uncle Julius, has a cornice with modillions and dentils, a swelled and ornamented frieze, an architrave with three fasciæ, divided by mouldings, and an Attic base.

The Maison Quarre, at Nismes, has a cornice with modillions and dentils, a flat frieze, an architrave with three fasciæ, divided by mouldings, and an Attic base.

Of the modern architects who treated of this order, Palladio makes the column nine and a half diameters high; one fifth of which he gives to the entablature, consisting of a cornice with modillions and dentils, a flat frieze, and an architrave with three fasciæ, divided by astragals: the base is Attic. The design of Scammozzi bears a general resemblance to that of Palladio, but his column has ten diameters in its altitude; his entablature is one fifth of this height; the cornice has modillions, the architrave consists of three fasciæ, divided by astragals, and the base is Attic. Serlio, following Vitruvius, has given this order an Ionic entablature, with dentils, and the same proportion of the capital; his column is nine diameters high, and has a Corinthian base. Vignola's Corinthian is a grand and beautiful composition, chiefly imitative of the three columns. He makes the column ten diameters and a half in height; the entablature is a fourth of that altitude, the cornice has modillions and dentils, the frieze is plain, the architrave of three fasciæ, divided by mouldings, and the base is Attic.

In the following table will be found the proportions of some of the principal examples of the Corinthian order; in examining which, it is to be recollected, that the several members are measured by the lower diameter of the shafts, which is divided into sixty parts, which are called minutes.

	Height of Column.		Height of Capital.	Archi-trave.	Frieze.	Cornice.
	Diam.	Min.	Min.	Min.	Min.	Min.
Portico of the Pantheon	9	$34\frac{1}{4}$	$67\frac{3}{4}$	$42\frac{3}{4}$	$39\frac{1}{2}$	54
Temple of Vesta, at Tivoli	9	$21\frac{3}{4}$	57	30	$37\frac{1}{2}$	$32\frac{1}{2}$
Temple of Antonius and Faustina	9	$36\frac{1}{2}$	$68\frac{3}{4}$	$43\frac{1}{2}$	$40\frac{2}{3}$	$52\frac{1}{2}$
Three Columns in the Campo Vaccino	10	$6\frac{5}{6}$	$66\frac{1}{2}$	$43\frac{1}{2}$	$43\frac{1}{3}$	$69\frac{5}{12}$
The Basilica of Antonius, at Rome	10	$11\frac{3}{4}$	$69\frac{1}{2}$	$43\frac{1}{2}$	$32\frac{1}{2}$	Missing.
The Arch of Constantine	9	37	$65\frac{3}{4}$	45	40	$58\frac{7}{12}$
Temple at Ephesus	10	15	64	48	$45\frac{1}{3}$	48
Temple at Jackly, near Mylassa	9	31	63	$43\frac{2}{3}$	40	Missing.
Pœile, at Athens	9	32	$64\frac{2}{5}$	$39\frac{3}{4}$	$34\frac{3}{4}$	$38\frac{3}{4}$
Arch of Adrian, at Athens	9	52	72	41	$38\frac{3}{4}$	46
The Incantada, at Salonica	9	31	$66\frac{3}{4}$	46	$41\frac{1}{2}$	$42\frac{1}{2}$
Palladio	9	30	70	38	$28\frac{1}{2}$	$47\frac{1}{2}$
Scammozzi	10		70	40	32	48
Serlio	9		60	30	37	39
Vignola	10		70	45	45	60

This example of the Corinthian order is taken from the temple of Jupiter Stator, at Rome, and is considered one of the most beautiful examples of the order.

A is a design of the base on a large scale.

CORINTHIAN CAPITAL.

PLATE XIX.

Projection of the Corinthian Capital.

Fig. 1 is the plan. Make the length of the diagonal of the abacus two diameters; the centre of each side is determined by the vertex of an equilateral triangle; the semi-plan is divided into eight equal parts, which being carried up perpendicularly to fig. 2, the elevation gives the centres of the leaves of which the projections are formed by those upon the plan, as is shown by dotted lines. To draw the faces of the abacus: With the distance *a b* describe the segments of a circle *a b, b c, c d* and *d a*. Fig. 3 shows the form and manner of raffling the leaves; fig. 3 being the front, and fig. 4 the side view. Fig. 5 is a design for a leaf differing from fig. 2, and was taken from the three columns in the Campo Vaccino. Fig. 6 is a design for the soffit, and fig. 7 the side view of a modillion.

COMPOSITE ORDER.

PLATE XX.

THE example here given is taken from the arch of Titus at Rome, erected soon after the destruction of Jerusalem, for the purpose of commemorating that event.

This order was first used by the Romans in their triumphal arches, to show their dominion over the nations which they had conquered, and was by them generally covered with a great profusion of enrichments. Although the capital, which is a distinguished feature in this order, is in the lower part Corinthian, and the upper part Ionic, it produced, nevertheless, a rich and martial effect, well adapted to the use to which it was put by the Romans; an effect which would be sought for in vain from the delicate Corinthian capital.

PEDESTALS.

PLATE XXI.

PEDESTALS are, I believe, a Roman invention; they are useful for supporting a colonnade or a pilastrade, and sometimes supply the office of a basement to a building. They consist of a base, die, and cornice.

In the original examples of Grecian architecture, we find the columns standing on the uppermost of three steps; a rule to which we know of but one existing exception, to be seen in the temple of Theseus, at Athens, which has but two steps. The Romans, however, when they raised the floors of their temples and other edifices high, were under the necessity of discontinuing the front stairs, lest they should prove inconvenient by occupying too much ground around the building, and of adopting the pedestal raised to a level with the top of the stairs, and projecting to the front of the steps which profiled on its sides.

Wherever pedestals are introduced, the grandeur of the order is diminished, as all the parts are proportionably reduced; yet they are indispensable in some situations.

In ancient Roman buildings, the proportions of pedestals are very variable; but some modern writers have endeavored to reduce them to a regular standard. Vignola would have them to be one third of the altitude of the column; but as this appeared to make them too high, Sir William Chambers reduced it to three tenths; but both ratios must be subject to variation, according to circumstances. Pedestals still lower are to be preferred.

As to the decorations of pedestals, projecting tablets are inadmissible. It is sometimes customary to adorn the dies with sunk pannels, surrounded with mouldings; and the pannels themselves are occasionally occupied by bass reliefs or inscriptions.

Pedestals should never be insulated, though the columns sustained by them be so. In the ancient theatres and amphitheatres, the inferior orders rested upon steps, while all the superior orders stood upon pedestals, which formed a parapet for raising the base of the order sufficiently high to be seen on a near approach to the building, and for the spectators to lean over; but they never exceeded the height necessary for the prevention of accident.

On Plate XXI. are four designs for pedestals, which may be used with the Tuscan, Doric, Ionic and Corinthian orders, their details being figured on the plate.

ARCADES.

PLATE XXII.

WHEN an aperture in a wall is too wide to be lintelled, it is arched over, and receives the appellation of an arcade, which term, in the plural number, indicates a continued range of such apertures. They are not so magnificent as colonnades, but are stronger, more solid, and less expensive.

In the construction of arcades, the piers require the utmost care to have them of sufficient strength to resist the pressure of the arches, particularly those at the extremities. In large arches, the key-stone should never be omitted, and they should be carried to the soffit of the architrave, where they would be useful in supporting the centre of the entablature, which would otherwise have too great a bearing. The altitude of arcades should never be much more nor much less than double their breadth. The breadth of the pier should seldom exceed two thirds, nor be less than one third of that of the arcade; and the angular one should have the addition of a third, or even a half more than the rest, according to the nature of the design. The impost should not be less than a ninth, nor more than a seventh of the breadth of the arch; and the archivolt not less than a tenth, nor more than an eighth, of the same breadth. The bottom of the keystone should be equal in breadth to that of the archivolt; and its length not less than one and a half, nor more than double its bottom breadth. Make the height of the impost moulding equal to the breadth of the impost.

FLUTES AND FILLETS.

PLATE XXIII.

FIG. 2 shows the manner of setting out the flutes on the column of the Doric order. A represents the size of the column at base, and B at the neck. Divide the circumference into twenty equal parts, that being the number of flutes for this column, and give one part to each flute; divide one part, as *a b*, into four parts; with three of these parts, and on 1, 2, 3, 4, 5, 6, 7, &c., describe the curves.

Fig. 1 shows the elevation of a part of the column, when fluted.

Fig. 5 shows a semi-plan, and fig. 4 an elevation of the Ionic column. Divide its circumference into twenty-four equal parts, and divide one of these twenty-fourth parts into four parts; with one and a half of these four parts, and on 1, 2, 3, 4, 5, 6, 7, 8, &c., describe the flutes, making each of them a half circle, so that each fillet is equal to one third of a flute.

Fig 3 shows the division of the flutes and fillets on a large scale.

Fig. 6 shows how to diminish a column after the Roman taste. Divide the shaft of the column into four parts, and leave the lower fourth undiminished; divide the remaining three fourths into six equal parts, as represented on the central line of the column. On A describe the circle *b e, d c;* make *e d* equal to the diameter of the column at the neck, and divide the circle *b e* into six equal parts ; draw lines parallel to *b c* through each of these divisions, cutting the circle on each side of the centre of the column ; then transfer the distances 1 1, 2 2, 3 3, 4 4, 5 5, in A, to 1 1, 2 2, 3 3, 4 4 and 5 5, from the central line of the column both ways, and through these parts trace the curved lines of each side the column.

PLATE XXIV.

To glue up the Shaft of a Column.

On Plate **XXIV.** is shown the method of gluing up the shaft of columns.

Draw the plans of the column intended to be made at both base and neck, as shown in fig. 1 and 2. In this example, I have made the column sixteen inches in diameter at the base, and have divided it into eight staves. If the sides of the column be straight, two inch plank will be sufficiently thick for the staves. Make the joints in a fillet, or between two flutes. It will be seen that the plans show the exact width of each end of the staves, and also the bevel of their edges, and the curve of the outside. After the staves are got out by an accurate plan and with great exactness, as they must be, or your work will be bad, proceed to glue the edges of two of them. When the glue is dry, glue in blocks on the inside, as shown in the plans at *c c c,* &c. Let the blocks be from fifteen to twenty inches long. Fit them exactly to the staves, and place the grain of the wood the same way as that of the column, so that, if the wood shrinks or swells, the joints will not open or be affected thereby. Proceed in the same manner until you come to the last stave ; then get out the blocks sufficiently wide to reach across the space left for the last stave ; then glue the block on to each of the adjoining staves, and when the glue is dry, proceed to glue in the last stave. As it is wider at the base than at the neck, an opportunity is offered to drive it up to a joint. Then, after working off the superfluous wood, and completing the flutes, give it a good coat of paint, to prevent its cracking or being affected in any way by the weather.

In making large columns, a greater number of staves will be required, and it will also be necessary that the planks be increased in thickness.

BALUSTRADES.

PLATE XXV.

BALUSTERS are sometimes of real use; as in stairs, windows, terraces, and on the sides of passages, open on one or both sides. At other times, they are merely ornamental; as when terminating the upper part of the front of a building, as a screen to conceal the whole or part of the roof, or as a finish to insulated triumphal arches. They consist of short pillars of a peculiar outline, standing upon a plinth, and covered with a small cornice. No remains of balusters have been found in any ancient buildings. In the theatres and amphitheatres of the Romans, the pedestals of the upper orders were always continued through the arcades, and served as parapets. The lower seats next to the arena in the amphitheatres, and those next to the orchestra in the theatres, were guarded by a parapet, called the podium. The top of the monument of Lysicrates, at Athens, is finished with a sort of parapet or ledge, composed of honey-suckles, solid behind, and open between every pier. Each plant is bordered with a curved head ; and the bottom of every interval, with an inverted curve. Balustrades are represented in the works of the earliest Italian writers, who might have seen them in the ruins of Roman structures; but none have been discovered in modern times. When a balustrade finishes a building, where an order is employed, its height should be proportioned to the architecture which it accompanies, but ought never to exceed that of the entablature on which it is placed, or be less than two thirds the height of the same. A good proportion, for balustrades of this kind, is to divide the whole given height into thirteen equal parts, and to make the height of the base equal to three of these parts, the height of the baluster to eight, and that of the cornice to two. The baluster may be divided into seven or eight parts in height, one of which will be the diameter at the base ; the one or the other, as the work which they accompany is light or heavy. The distance between the balusters should not exceed half the breadth of their plinth, nor be less than one third. On stairs and inclined planes, the same proportions are to be observed as on horizontal surfaces.

I have given four designs for balusters, which are figured on the plate, as to both height and projection, so as to be made plain to inspection. The contour of the mouldings has been carefully drawn, and it is believed that they will appear graceful, if imitated.

ANTÆ.

Though the earlier architects of Greece were either unacquainted with the use of pilasters, or refused to introduce them into their designs, they frequently placed a kind of square pillars at the ends of their walls, which they called antæ, and which sometimes projected to a considerable distance from the principal front, forming the pronaos, or vestibulum. The breadth of these antæ was always much less on the flanks of temples, than on the front; and sometimes they had columns between them, in which case the return within the pronaos was of equal breadth with the front. The capitals of the antæ never correspond with those of the columns, though they always retain some characteristic marks by which the order may be distinguished.

PILASTERS.

PILASTERS differ from columns in having their horizontal sections of a rectangular figure, whilst the sections of columns are either complete circles, or sections of circles equal to or greater than semicircles. They are probably of Roman origin; there being but few Grecian buildings, and those of the later ages, (except the monument of Thrasyllus,) in which they are repeated at regular intervals, as in the monument of Philopapus; but of their application in Roman works we have numberless instances.

When ranged with columns under the same entablature, or behind a row of columns, they have their bases and capitals like those of the columns, with the corresponding parts at the same heights: when placed at the angles of buildings, the breadth of the return is equal to that of the front. The trunks, also, have frequently the same diminution as the shafts of columns; as in the arches of Septimius Severus and of Constantine, the frontispiece of Nero, and the temple of Mars Ultor at Rome. In these cases, the top of the trunk is equal to the soffit of the architrave, the upright face of which rests on the capital, in the same perpendicular with the top of the pilaster. When the pilaster is undiminished, and of the same breadth as the bottoms of the columns, the face of the architrave, resting on the capital, retreats within the head of the trunk, as in the Pantheon of Agrippa.*

Pilasters may be either plain or fluted, without regard to the columns. Thus, in the portico of the Pantheon, the columns are plain and the pilasters fluted; but in that of Septimius Severus, the former are fluted and the latter plain; the architects seeming to be governed by no other rule than their taste. The angles, or coins, of fluted pilasters, are frequently strengthened with a bead, as in the Pantheon, and the flutes are generally of a semicircular section. Sometimes the faces of pilasters are sunk within a margin, and the pannels charged with foliage, or other ornaments.

When placed on the front or outside of a building, pilasters should project one fourth of their breadth at the bottom; but in the interior, or behind a row of columns, they should not project more than one eighth of that breadth.

Pilasters are not only ornamental to a building, but they also tend to strengthen it greatly; to which we may add that they become an object of economy, as being less expensive than columns. In situations where they are either placed behind a range of columns, or for the support of the extremes of an entablature across an opening, they are also more concordant with the walls to which they are attached.

Clustered pilasters, or those which have both exterior and interior angles, with their planes parallel and perpendicular to the front, may be executed with good effect when the order is plain, as in the Tuscan; but in the Doric, Ionic and Corinthian orders, where triglyphs and capitals meet but imperfectly in the interior angles, such a junc-

* See Explanation of Plate VI.

Fig. 2.

Fig. 4.

Fig. 3.

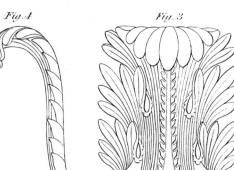

Fig. 5.

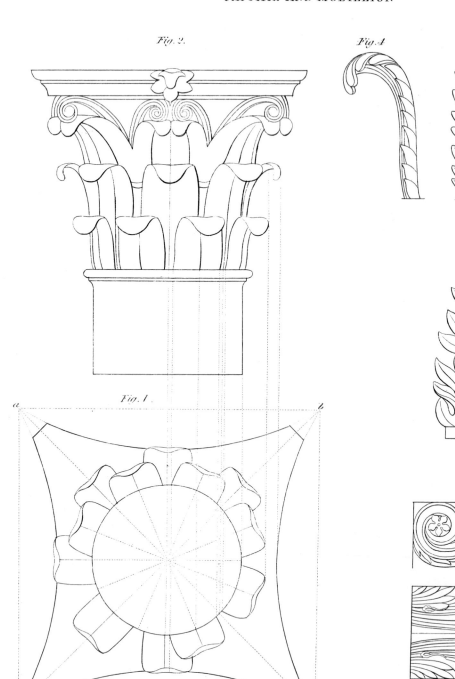

Fig. 1.

Fig. 7.

Fig. 6.

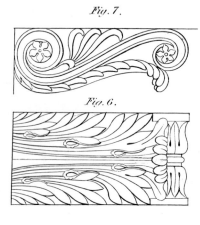

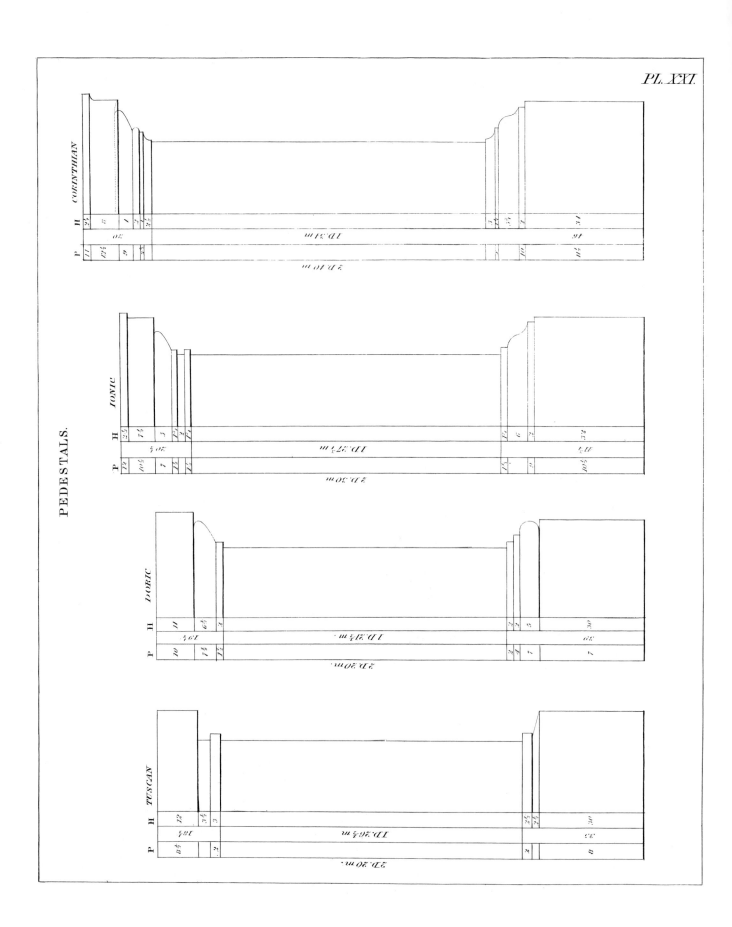

PEDESTALS.

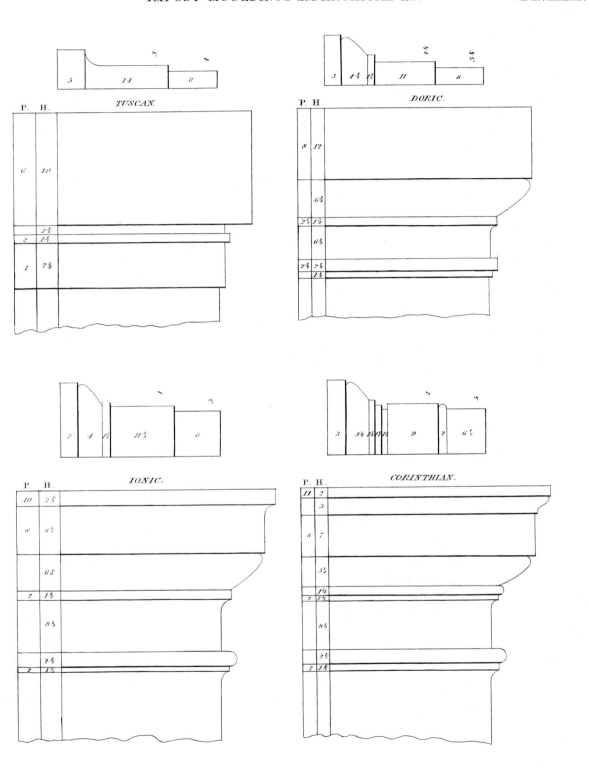

PL. XXIII.

Fig. 1

Fig. 2

Fig. 3

Fig. 4

Fig. 5

Tuscan Column.

7 Diameters

Fig. 6

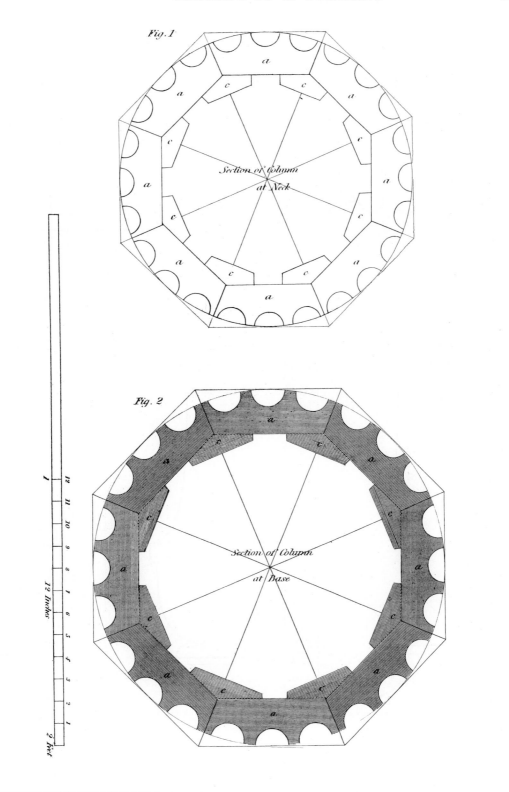

Fig. 1

Section of Column
at Neck

Fig. 2

Section of Column
at Base

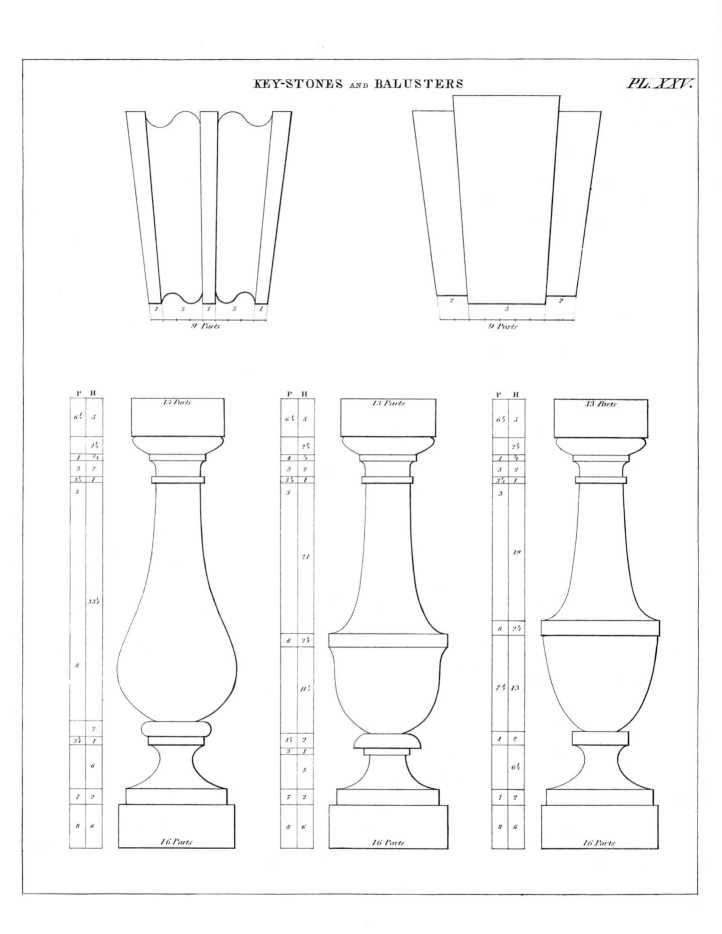

tion should be avoided as much as possible. The same may be observed of Ionic and Corinthian capitals of half pilasters, meeting each other in the interior angles of rooms. In the Ionic order, a difference must be made between the capitals of pilasters and of columns; for, in the latter, the projection of the ovolo is greater than that of the volutes: but, the horizontal section of the ovolo being circular, the ovolo is bent behind the hem or border of the volutes. It therefore becomes necessary either to give the ovolo but a small projection, or to make it so prominent in the front that its extremities may appear to retire behind the border of the volutes.

COLONNADE.

COLONNADE, a range of attached or insulated columns, supporting an entablature, is named according to the number of columns supporting the entablature: tetrastyle, when there are four; hexastyle, when six; octostyle, when eight; and decastyle, when ten.

The intervals between the columns, measured by their inferior diameter, are called the intercolumniation, whence the area between every two columns is termed the intercolumn.

The intercolumniation is of five denominations, viz.: the aræostyle, or thinly set, when the columns are at the distance of four diameters; the diastyle, when they are at three diameters; the eustyle, when at two and a quarter; the systyle, when at two; and the pycnostyle, or thickly set, when at the distance of one diameter and a half. Of these, the eustyle was in most general request among the ancients; and though, in modern buildings, both the eustyle and diastyle are employed, the former has obtained a marked preference. The pycnostyle is frequently rejected from want of room.

The intercolumniations of the Doric order are regulated by the number of triglyphs, one of which is placed over every intermediate column. When there is one triglyph over the interval, it is called monotriglyph; when there are two, it is called ditriglyph; and so on, according to the progression of the Greek numerals. The intercolumniation of the Grecian Doric is rarely any other than the monotriglyph, there being but two deviations from it at Athens, in the Doric portico and in the prophylæa; and even in these instances, the exception applies only to the middle intercolumniations, which are ditriglyph, and were necessary from their situation, being opposite to the principal entrances. Indeed, from the massive and bold character of the Grecian Doric, the monotriglyph succeeded best; but in the Roman Doric it would be inconvenient, because the passage between the columns would be too narrow, especially in small buildings; and therefore the ditriglyph is to be preferred.

When the solid parts of the masonry of a range of arcades are decorated with the orders, the intercolumns necessarily become wide, and the intercolumniation is regulated by the breadth of the arcades and of the piers. Vignola used the same intercolumniation in all his orders, and, though this practice is condemned by some, it is founded upon a right principle, as it preserves a constant ratio between the columns and the intervals.

Coupled, grouped, or clustered columns, seem not to have been used by the ancients.

The moderns seldom employ more than one row of columns in either external or internal colonnades; for in double rows the back range destroys the perspective regularity of that of the front; and the rays of light, proceeding from both ranges, produce confusion.

Pilasters, placed behind a row of insulated columns, are liable to the same objection, except that the relief is stronger, owing to the rotundity of the one being contrasted with the flat surface of the other.

In buildings upon a small scale, the intercolumniations, or, at least, the central one, must be broader than the positive dimensions of the pillars would admit.

ORDERS UPON ORDERS.

In placing one order above another, we shall be naturally led, by the known laws of gravity, to give the strongest and heaviest the lower place, and the weakest and lightest the upper. Symmetry and strength will likewise direct us to keep all their axes in the same vertical line.

In columns of equal diameters, the altitudes increase from the Tuscan, by the gradations of the Doric and Ionic, to the Corinthian. In this progression, we perceive that the Tuscan is stronger than the Doric, the Doric than the Ionic, and the Ionic than the Corinthian: consequently, if the Doric be the lowest order, the succeeding one must be the Ionic; if a third be added, it must be the Corinthian.

When a front of a building is to have two or more orders in the altitude, the succession must be complete, or the symmetry will be destroyed by the abrupt contrast of the parts. In attached columns, the superior may be permitted to recede, without danger either of greatly offending the eye, or of impairing the strength of the structure. But when the stories of orders are insulated, the axes of the superior and inferior columns must be kept in the same vertical lines.

The first and second orders should stand on plinths, as likewise the

third, when there is one; the point of view regulating those of the
upper stories. In this case, pedestals should be omitted in the upper orders; but if there be one, or a balustrade under the windows,
the base and cornice should have but a small projection, and be continued to profile upon the sides of the columns.

When stories of arcades are raised one upon another, and the piers
decorated with orders, the inferior columns should stand on plinths,
and those of the upper stories on pedestals, that the arches may receive a due proportion.

In some cases, instead of employing several orders one above
another, the ground floor of a building is made in the form of a basement, on which is placed the order by which the principal story is
decorated.

PEDIMENTS.

THESE ornaments probably owe their origin to the inclined roofs
of the primitive huts. They consist of a horizontal cornice, representing a tie beam, and two others of equal inclination over it, indic-
ative of rafters; or the latter are exchanged for an arched one. The
surface included within these cornices is called a tympanum; which,
of course, is either a triangle or the segment of a circle.

In the ancient buildings of Greece, we find only the triangular pediment; but in those of Rome, both triangular and circular are to be
met with; and in rows of openings, or niches, both kinds are employed in alternate succession,—though they seem to have preferred
the triangular form for doors, windows and gates, and to have applied the circular pediment to the covering of large or small bodies
promiscuously.

Pediments, among the Romans, were exclusively appropriated to sacred edifices, till Cæsar obtained leave of the senate to cover his house with a painted roof, after the manner of the temples.

The ancients introduced but few pediments into their buildings, even the Romans usually contenting themselves with a single one to adorn the middle or principal part.

Vitruvius has given the following direction for finding the pitch of a pediment. "Divide the space between the extremities of the cymatium of the corona into nine equal parts, and take one for the height of the tympanum." This rule has been considered as too low: but it must be recollected, that of the octostyle portico of the Pantheon, at Athens, is nearly of the proportion here described; that of the hexastyle portico of the temple of Theseus is about an eighth; that of the Ionic temple on the Illyssus, and of the Doric portico, are about one seventh; and the tympanum of the pediment over the door of the Tower of the Winds, is about one fifth of the span; all which edifices are Athenian.

From this comparison, a kind of reciprocal ratio seems to exist between the extension of the base of the tympanum and its height; and, indeed, were a fixed ratio applied to both large and small pediments, the latter would frequently consist of a cornice only, without any tympanum. It is therefore with good reason that the pitch of small pediments is made higher than large ones.

When pediments are to be covered with either slates or shingles, they cannot with safety be less in height than two ninths of their base.

It is an observation of Vitruvius, that " the Greeks never used mutules, modillions, or dentils, in the front, wherein the end of the roof appears, because the ends of the rafters and of the laths, which support the tiles, only appear at the eaves of the building; and as mutules and dentils originated from the projecting ends of the rafters and laths, it would have been absurd to introduce them into the pediment, where the exemplars are themselves to be seen." We find in the Grecian remains, that, though neither mutules, dentils nor modillions are employed in the sloping sides, mutules are constantly used in the horizontal cornice. In edifices of the period of Roman domination in Greece, indeed, we sometimes may observe them in the sloping cornices; but they must be considered as innovations. At Rome, we find examples of modillions in the Pantheon, and in the frontispiece of Nero; and in the temple of Fortune dentils are used. In the inclined cornices, the sides of the modillions and dentils are planes perpendicular to the horizon, and to the front of the edifice, and in the same vertical planes of those of the horizontal cornice.

It is to be observed, that the two uppermost mouldings of the cornice are always omitted in the horizontal one of a pediment; that part of the profile being directed upwards, to finish the inclined cornices.

The face of the tympan is always placed on a line perpendicular with the face of the frieze.

ATTICS.

AMONG the Athenians, it was a rule to conceal the roofs of their buildings; for which purpose they crowned their cornices with low square pillars, of a form nearly approaching that of a pedestal, which have obtained the appellation of Attics, from the country in which they were first or chiefly employed, though no remains are now to be discovered among the ruins of the ancient city of Athens.

Roman Attics are to be seen in the remains of the triumphal arches, and in the piazza of Nerva. In the arch of Constantine, the columns are surmounted with pedestals as high as the base of the Attic, upon which are placed insulated statues. At Thessalonica, there is an Attic over a Corinthian colonnade, with breaks forming dwarf pilasters over the columns, as in the arch of Constantine. The Attic, which is carried round the two courts of the great temple of Balbec, is also broken into dwarf pilasters over the columns and pilasters of the order; which dwarf pilasters are surmounted with blocking courses, wherein statues are supposed to have stood.

In all these remains, the Attics are disproportional; some of them being nearly one half of the height of the order. The moderns make their height equal to that of the entablature; and the proportion of the members may be regulated as in the cases of pedestals.

NICHES.

THESE, among the Romans, have either a circular or rectangular plan. The heads of those of the circular kind are generally spherical.

The plans of niches with cylindrical backs should be semicircular, when the thickness of the walls will admit of it; and the depth of those upon rectangular plans should be half of their breadth, or as deep as may be necessary for the statues they are to contain. Their heights depend upon the character of the statues, or on the general form of groups introduced ; yet seldom exceeding twice and a half their width, nor being less than twice.

In point of decorations, niches admit of all such as are applicable to windows ; and, whether their heads be horizontal, cylindrical or spherical, the enclosure may be rectangular. In antique remains, we frequently meet with tabernacles as ornaments, disposed with alternate and arched pediments ; the character of the architecture should be similar to that placed in the same range with them.

Niches are sometimes disposed between columns and pilasters, and sometimes ranged alternately, in the same level with windows. In either case, they may be ornamented or plain, as the space will admit ; but in the latter, they should be of the same dimensions with the aperture of the windows. When the intervals between the columns or pilasters happen to be very narrow, niches had better be omitted than have a disproportionate figure, or be of a diminutive size.

When intended for statues, vases, or other works of sculpture, they should be contrived to exhibit them to the best advantage ; and, consequently, the plainer the niche the better will it answer the design, as every species of ornament, whether of mouldings or sculpture, has a tendency to confuse the outline.

VASES.

PLATE XXVI.

On this plate are a series of designs for vases. When vases are used on pedestals, posts to fences, and for such like purposes, their largest diameter may be made equal to the diameter of the pedestal, or post, on which they are to be placed, or from that size to one fourth

DESIGNS FOR URNS

DESIGN FOR A FRONT DOOR

PL. XXVII.

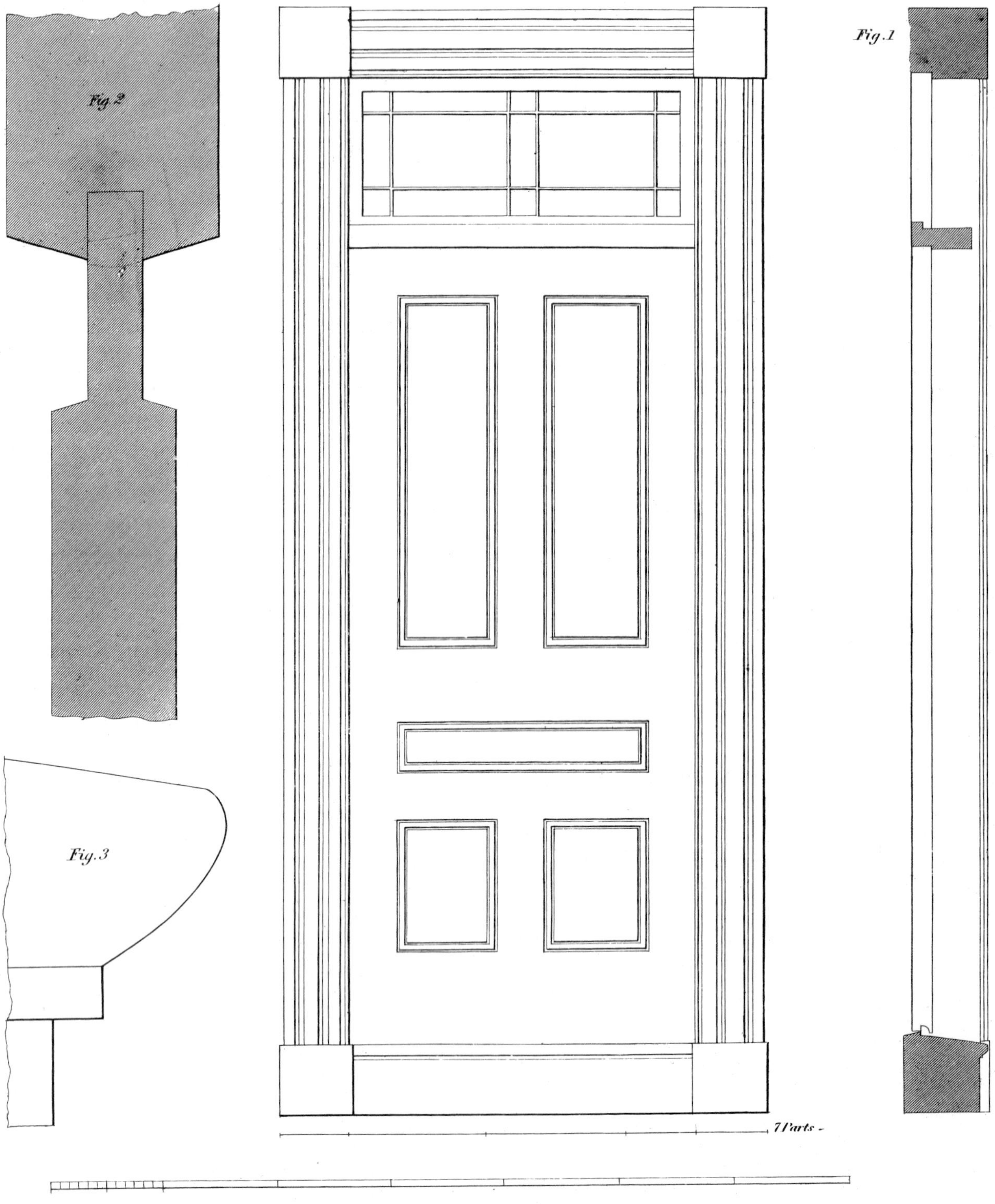
Fig. 1
Fig. 2
Fig. 3
7 Parts

DESIGN FOR A FRONT DOOR CASE.   *PL. XXVIII.*

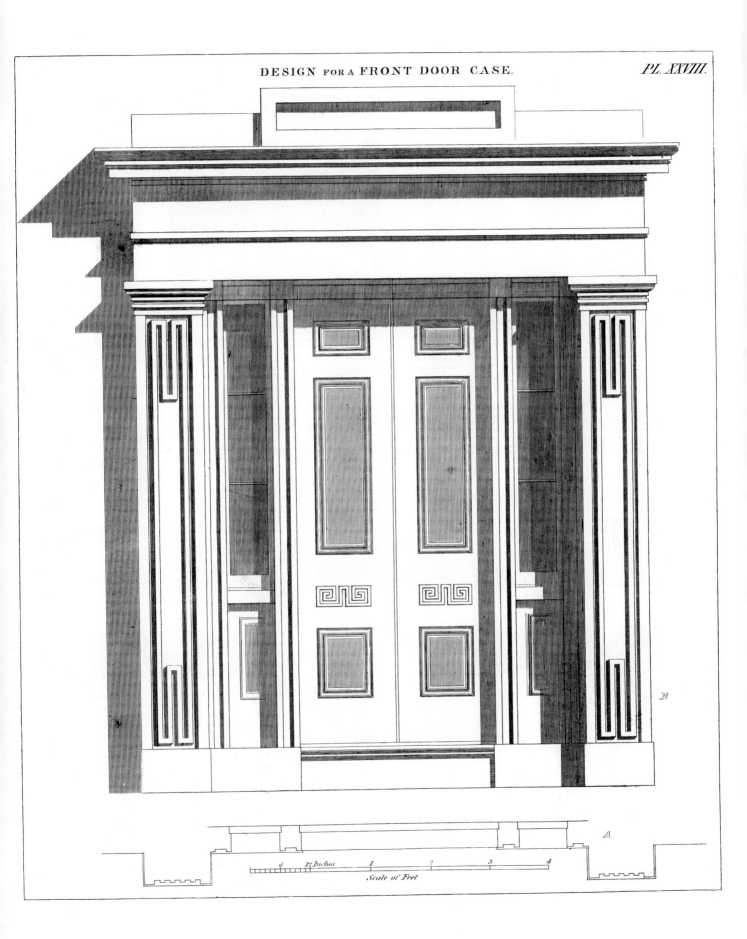

6 1½ Inches   1   2   3   4

Scale of Feet.

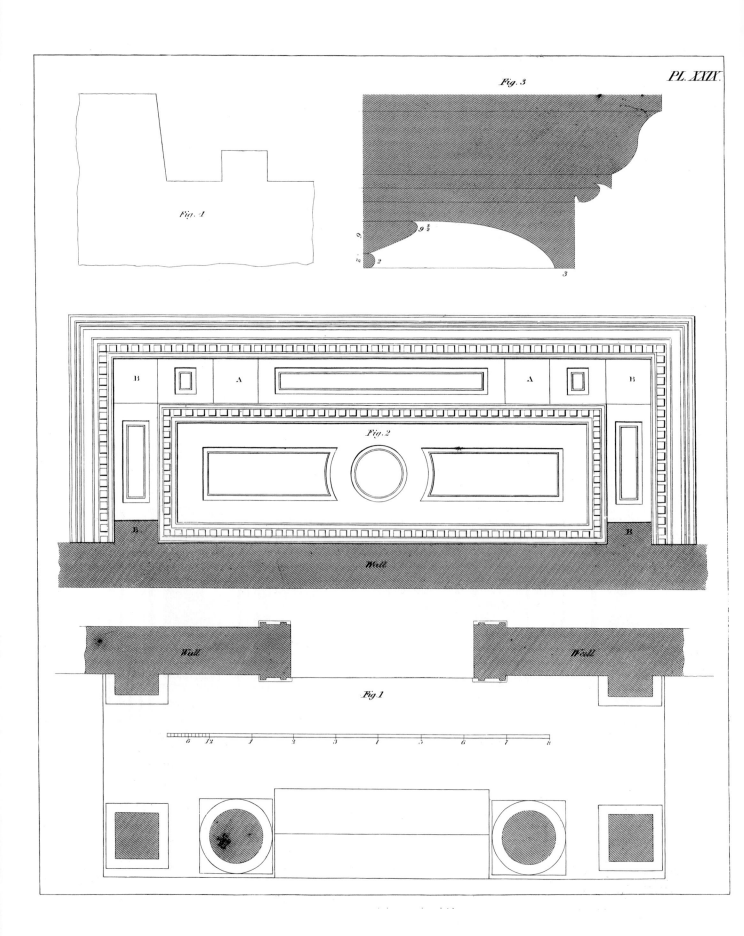

Fig. 3

Fig. 4

B A A B

Fig. 2

Wall

B B

Wall Wall

Fig 1

part less, as judgment may dictate. As the heights and projections of all the members to each vase are figured on the plate, I trust that, by an examination, they will be clearly understood.

FRONTISPIECE.

PLATE XXVII.

On this plate is a design for a frontispiece of the most simple kind. It may be used with success where the facade of the house is very plain. To proportion the architrave, divide the width of the door into five equal parts, and make the width of the architrave equal to one of these parts.

Fig. 1 shows an elevation of the jamb to the door, and also a section of the threshold and impost between the door and sash.

Fig. 2 shows a section of a part of the stile and panel of the door, at full size.

Fig. 3 shows the moulding of the threshold, also at full size.

A scale of feet and inches is annexed, by which any part of the design may be measured.

PLATE XXVIII.

On this plate is a plan and elevation of a Venetian entrance, decorated with pilasters and an entablature, which are so plain and simple, that they may be easily wrought in stone. The pilasters in this example are seven diameters in height; but they may be made seven and a half, or eight, when a lighter proportion is desired. The

capital and entablature are taken from Plate **XIV**. The other parts
of the design may be measured by the scale of feet and inches an
nexed.

_____

IONIC PORTICO.

PLATES XXIX. and XXX.

On Plate **XXIX.** in fig. **1**, is represented the plan, which clearly
shows how to place the columns and pilasters of the portico.

Fig. **2** shows the soffit of the cornice, architrave and ceiling, inverted. **A A** is that part of the soffit of the architrave which is directly over the capital of the columns; and **B B B B** that directly
over the capital of the pilasters.

Fig. **4** shows a section of a part of the panelling.

On Plate **XXX.** is shown the elevation, the proportions of which
are taken from the Ionic Order, Example No. 3, Plate **XII.**

On Plate **XXIX.** fig. **3**, is a section of a cornice, suitably constructed for the inclined sides of a pediment. I know of no determinate rule by which the general proportions of a frontispiece can be
ascertained, in all situations. He who takes the most comprehensive
view of all the circumstances connected with the building to which
the frontispiece is to be attached, will be the most likely to produce
the most successful effects, by a true proportion.

The frontispiece must, in some degree, be in proportion to the
house it is to accompany, with respect to both size and character.
If the house be large, and highly ornamented, the frontispiece must
also be large, and the ornaments partake of the character of the
house.

Fig. 2

Fig. 1

a

Stone

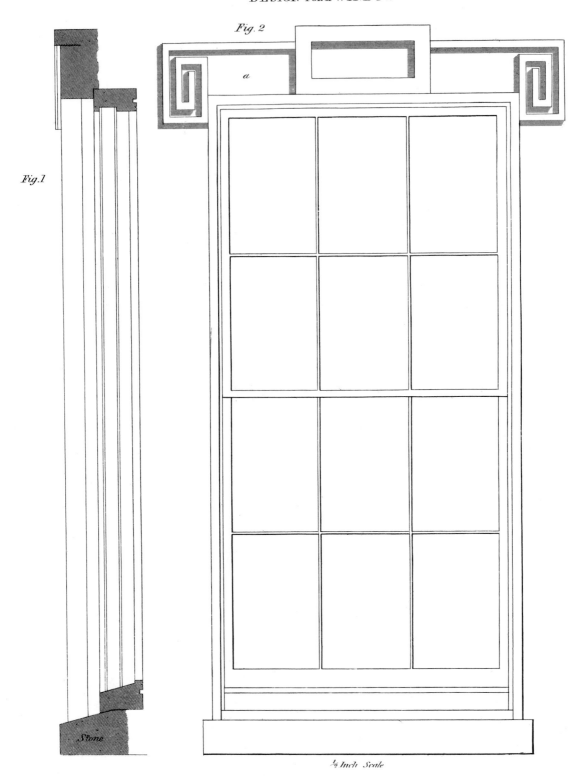

⅓ Inch Scale

WINDOWS.

––––

PLATE XXXI.

THE size of the apertures depends chiefly on the size and destination of the building. The height ought to be about twice their breadth; and the breadth of the piers is generally from one to one and a half the breadth of the window: but this proportion must often be departed from, in order to admit of external and internal decorations. The sills of windows should, in common edifices, be placed at a height of from two feet two, to two feet six inches from the floor. In elegant apartments, the sills are frequently placed at a height of seven or eight inches from the floor, and, in that case, the windows are made in height more than twice the breadth. It is common in different stories to have different heights to windows, decreasing in the upper stories, until in the Attics they are often made in height equal to their breadth. Windows ought always to be placed vertically, one over the other, and not too near the angles of the building. Fig. 2 represents a sash, frame, window cap and sill, set into a brick wall. Fig. 1 shows a section through the sash, frame, cap and sill, and a part of the brick wall.

A stone cap over a window indicates strength, its object being to support the bricks which rest upon it. All embellishments, therefore, that are made on its front, must project from a vertical line of the wall. Never suffer any of the cuttings to go beyond this line, because that would indicate weakness, and, of course, would be highly improper.

DORMER WINDOW

PLATE XXXII.

On this plate is shown a design for a dormer window, suitably constructed for being placed on the roof of a building. It is drawn on a scale large enough to make it plain, without further explanation. Fig. 1 shows a front, and fig. 2 a side elevation.

Fig. 3 and 4, on the same plate, show designs of a species of the guiloche, which may sometimes be used with good effect on fences, railings, &c.

FRONT FENCES.

PLATE XXXIII.

On this plate are three designs for fences, suitable for the enclosure of a country residence, which may be made of wood, when iron is not to be obtained, or when expense is to be avoided: also two designs for gates, to be made of the same material. Mouldings do not form any part of the composition of these designs. Their construction is bold and simple, and will, if well executed, produce a more chaste and pleasing effect than if the cornice, top rail and base were composed of small, trifling mouldings, and is the means of saving considerable expense.

It is not supposed that the size of these examples will suit all situations. There are many situations which require the size of

DESIGN for a WINDOW

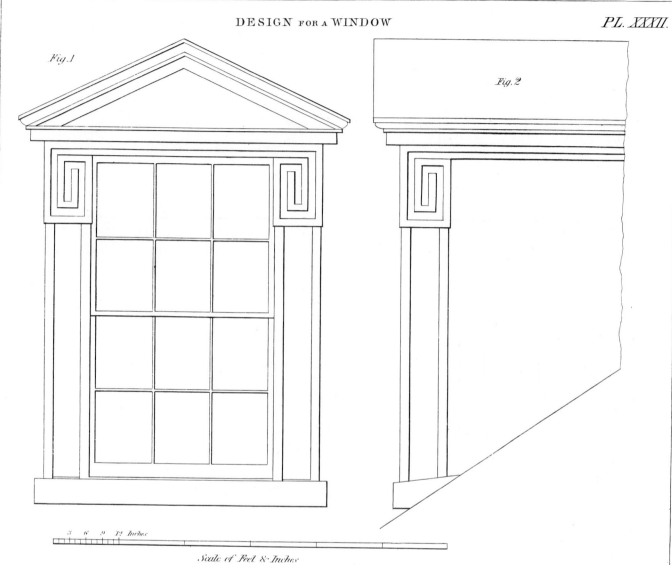

Fig.1

Fig.2

3 6 9 12 Inches

Scale of Feet & Inches

Fig.3

Fig.4

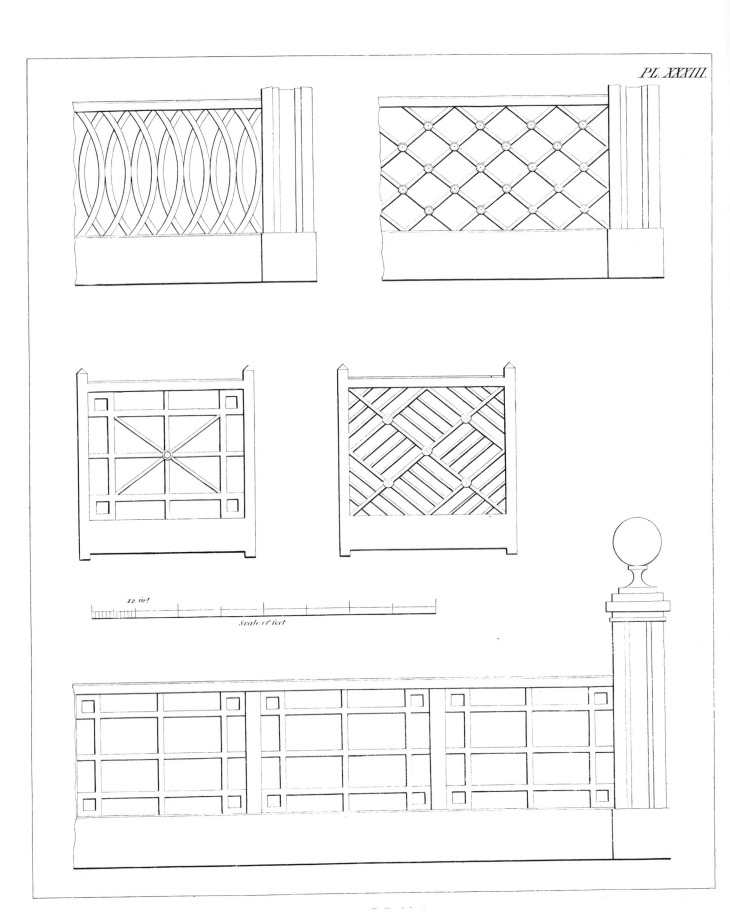

12 in.

Scale of feet

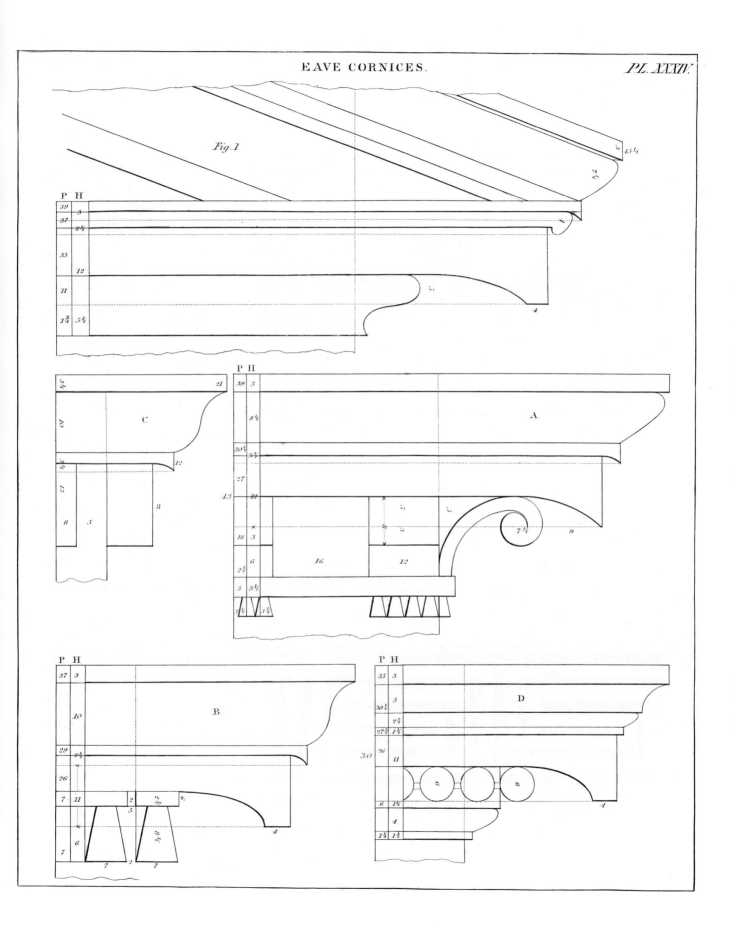

Fig.1

Fig. 1.

Fig. 2

front fences to be varied; as, for instance, when the house is very large, and located on an elevated piece of ground, and at a considerable distance from the road : in this case, the fence should be of the largest dimensions. But if the house be small, and so situated as to have the fence near it, the fence ought then to be small and low, so that it may not appear as a principal in the structure.

EAVE CORNICES.

PLATE XXXIV.

On this plate are four designs for eave cornices. To proportion their height, divide the height of the building, on which A is to be used, into twenty-four equal parts, and make the height of the cornice on the wall equal to one of these parts. If B or D is to be used, divide the height of the building into twenty-five parts, and make the height of the cornice equal to one of them. If C is to be used, divide the height into thirty equal parts, and give one of them to the height of the cornice.

PLATE XXXV.

On this plate are designs for eave cornices with friezes. In determining their height and proportion, judgment is to be used. If a house have a front of forty or fifty feet, it will be necessary to make the cornice somewhat larger than if the front only occupy a space of twenty or twenty-five feet. As a general proportion, give to the height of the cornice on the wall, without the frieze, from one twenty-fifth to one thirtieth of the height of the wall.

STUCCO CORNICES.

PLATES XXXVI. and XXXVII.

On these plates are designs for stucco cornices. What has heretofore been said with regard to the proportions of columns and cornices, will apply equally well here. There are many circumstances which ought materially to affect the size of cornices in rooms of the same height; such as the size of the room, and the style of the finish of the other parts of it. If the finish generally be light, the cornice ought also to be light; and if the finish of the room be composed of large, bold parts, make the cornice conformable thereto.

As stucco cornices occupy more space on the ceiling than on the vertical walls, I have thought it more proper to determine their projection than their height; and more particularly so, as, in many situations, a very small height only can be had. In such cases, the defect can in some degree be remedied by adding to the projection. As a general rule, give to the projection of the cornice five eighths of an inch for each foot in the height. If the room be ten feet in height, make the cornice project six and a quarter inches, or fifty eighths of an inch; then divide that distance into as many parts as are contained in the projection of the cornice you intend to make use of, and give those parts to the different members of the cornice, in both height and projection, as figured on the plate.

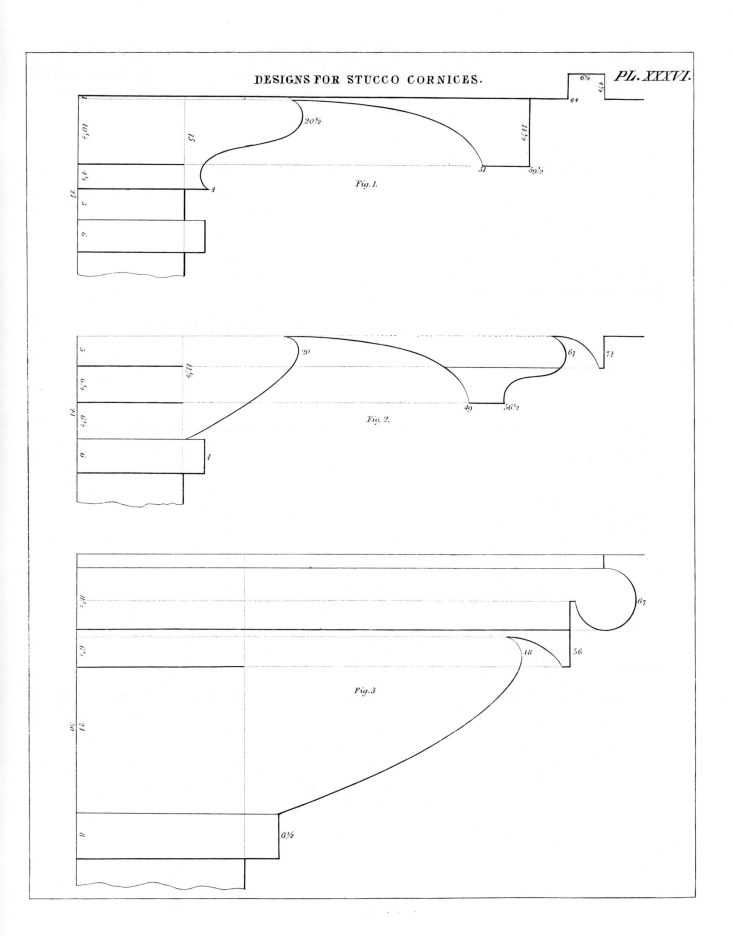

DESIGNS FOR STUCCO CORNICES.

PL. XXXVI.

Fig. 1.

Fig. 2.

Fig. 3.

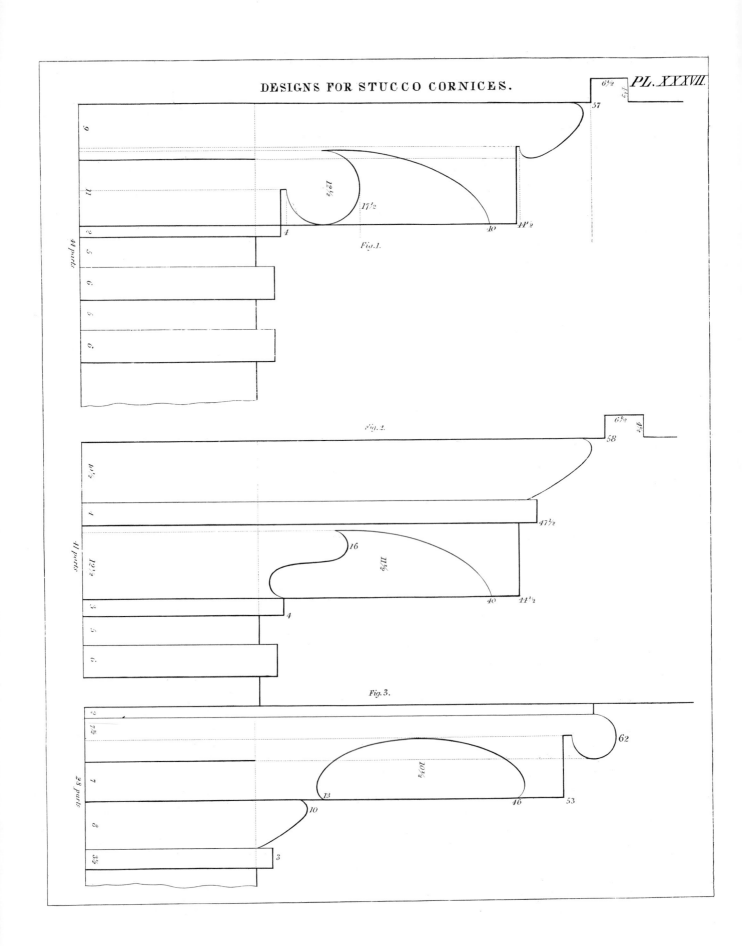

Fig. 1.

Fig. 2.

Fig. 3.

PL. XXXVII.

FINISHING. WINDOWS.

———

PLATE XXXVIII.

FIG. 1 shows a section of part of a brick wall, sash frame, window shutters, back lining, rough furrings, stucco, grounds and architrave. A, top of stone sill; E, top of wooden sill to sash frame; *a*, outside casing; *c*, pulley stile; *h*, ovolo; *b* back side casing next to bricks; *d*, inside casing to which the shutters are hung; *e*, parting strip between weights; *q*, *r*, weights; *f*, parting bead; *g*, inside bead to sash frame; *l*, back lining; *m*, rough furrings; *n*, grounds; *o*, stucco; *p*, architrave; and *i*, *k*, shutters.

Fig. 2 is a section of the cap to a sash frame. *c*, edge of outside casing; *b*, parting slip; *a*, inside bead.

Fig. 3. *g*, section of sill to sash frame; *i*, back under window; *h*, bead connected with sill and back; *d*, inside bead; *e*, parting slip; *f*, face casing.

Fig. 4 shows a section of the meeting rails, and parts of the upright bars of the sash, drawn at full size. B is a section of a sash bar, and C and D are sections of the stile, the mouldings, and part of a panel to shutters, also drawn at full size.

INSIDE DOORS.

PLATE XXXIX.

Doors are generally varied in their dimensions, according to the height of the story, and magnitude of the building in which they are used. The aperture of those of the smallest dimensions must be of a size sufficient to allow a man to pass easily through them: the smallest door cannot, therefore, be much less than two feet six inches wide, by six feet six inches high; nor should they be more than three feet eight inches in breadth, by eight feet in height, in private houses. When folding doors are used for the purpose of connecting rooms by large apertures, it will be advisable to make them double the width of the other doors, and very often to exceed that width; their height ought in general to exceed that of the other doors, in the same room, by twelve or fifteen inches. A good proportion for small doors is three to seven, and for very large ones one to two; for rooms about sixteen by eighteen or twenty feet, and ten to twelve feet high, a good proportion for the doors will be three by seven feet. Fig. 4 is a design of a door with five panels, without mouldings, as is shown by fig. 1, which represents a section of the stile and panel at large. Fig. 3 is a design for a door with eight panels; and fig. 2 shows a section of the moulding, a part of the panel, and also a part of the stile, drawn at full size. The doors are drawn from a scale of one inch to a foot.

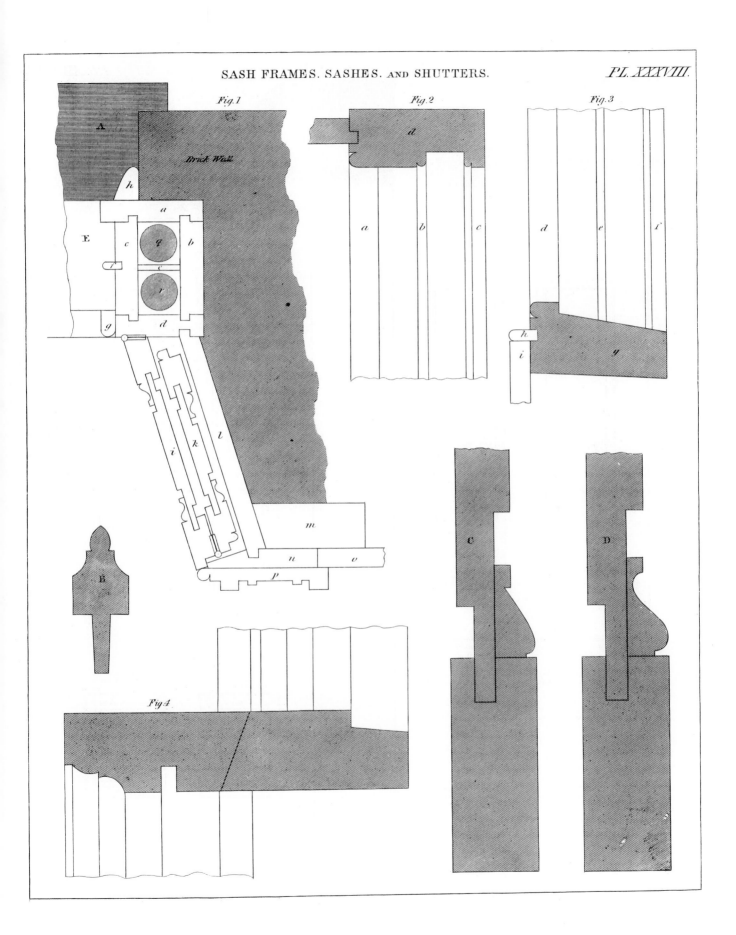

Fig.1

Fig.2

Fig.3

Fig.4

DESIGNS FOR DOORS.   PL. XXXIX.

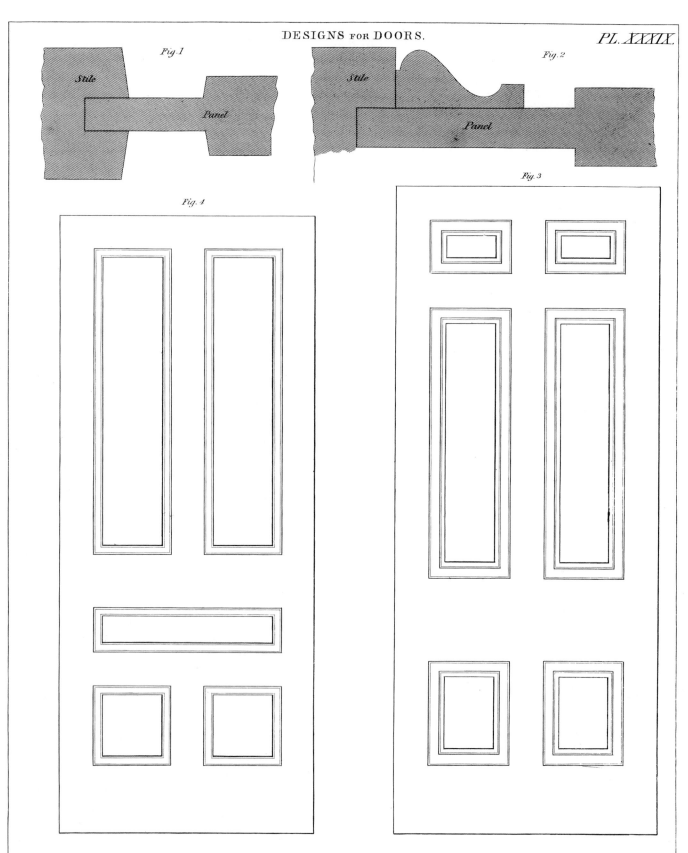

Fig. 1

Stile

Panel

Fig. 2

Stile

Panel

Fig. 3

Fig. 4

Scale — 1 Inch to a Foot.

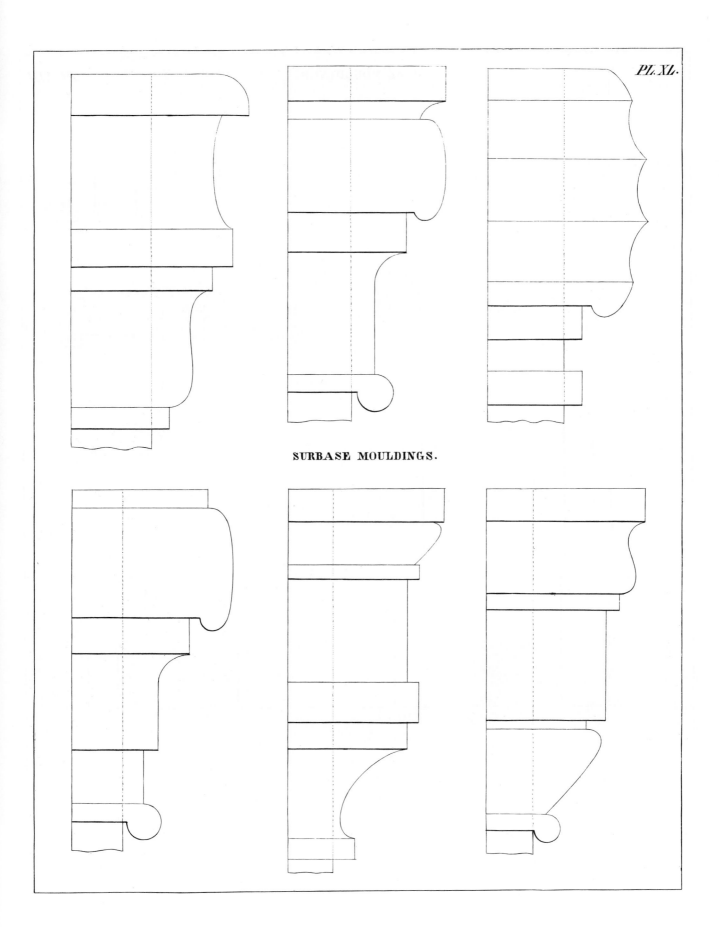

SURBASE MOULDINGS.

PL. XL.

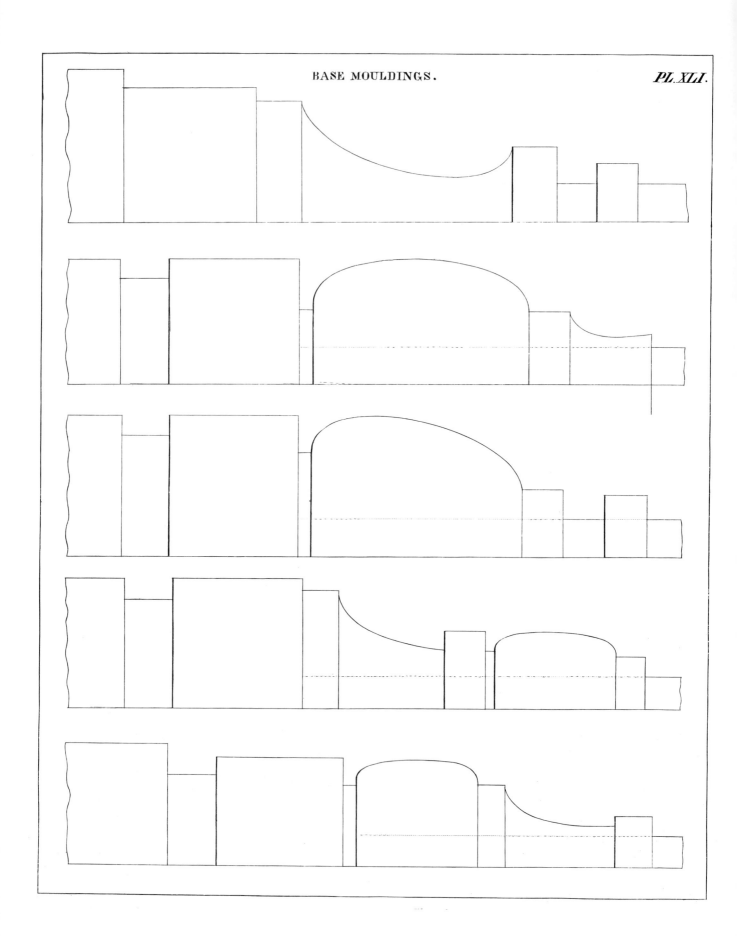

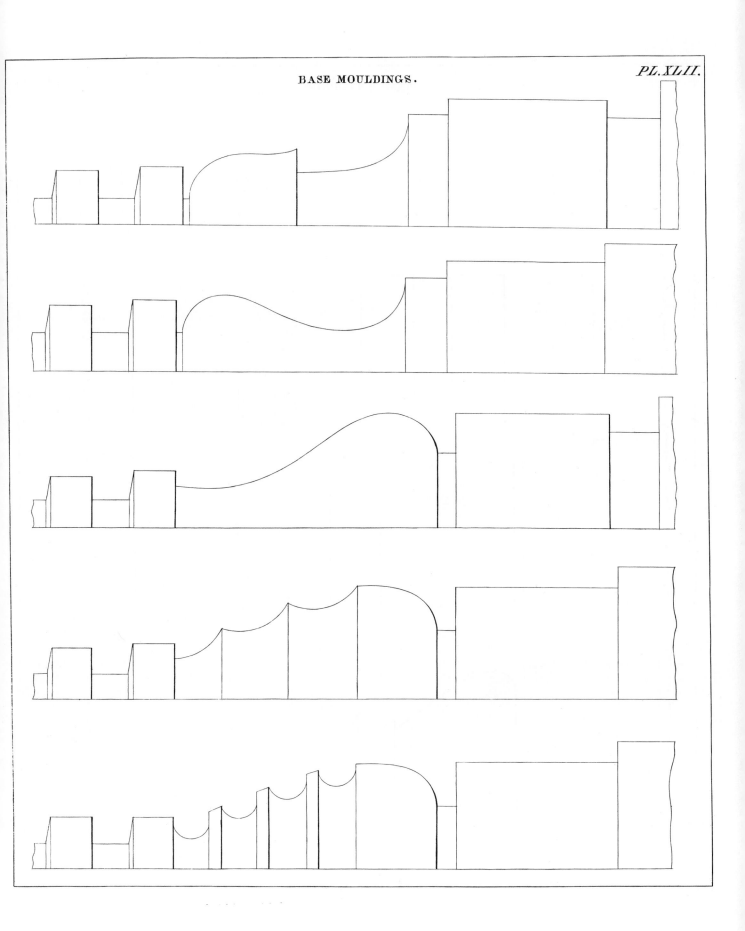

BASE MOULDINGS

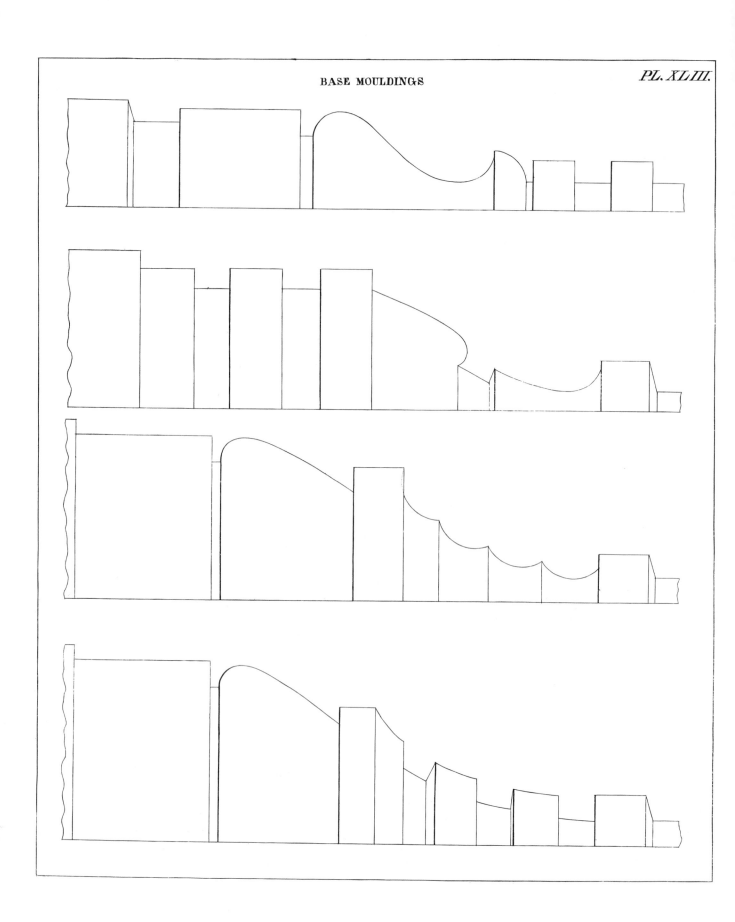

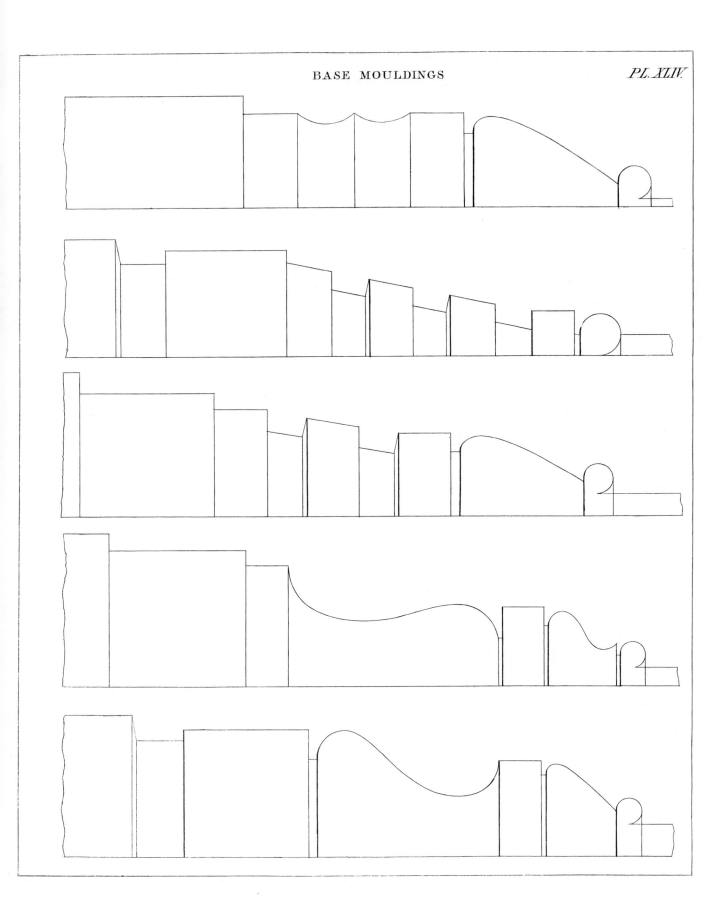

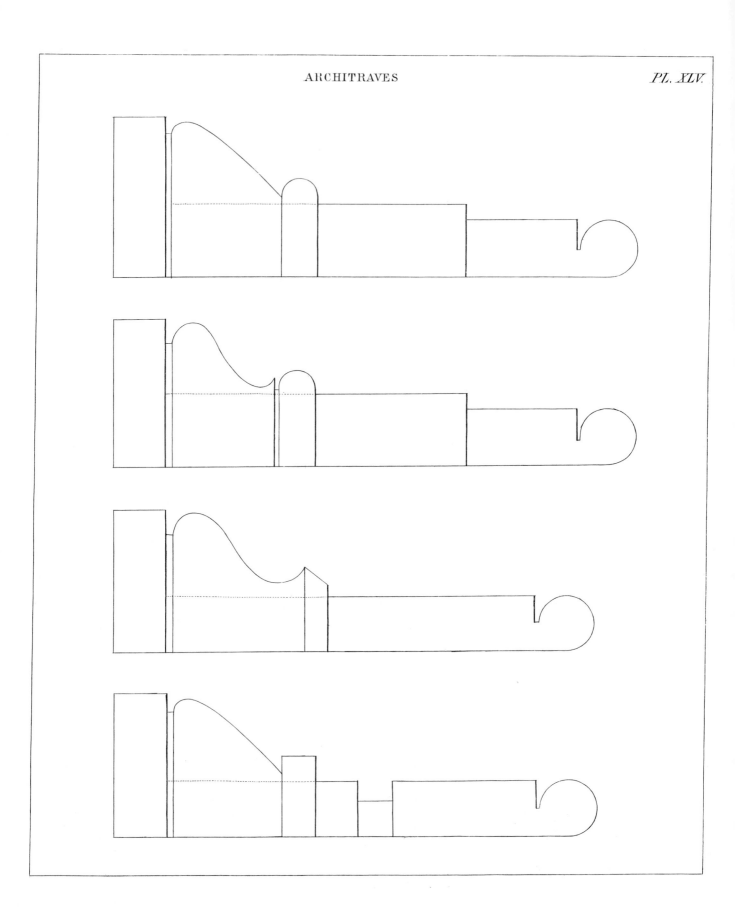

SUR-BASE MOULDINGS.

PLATE XL.

On this plate are six designs for sur-base mouldings, drawn at full size for practice. I have given these designs a place here, although the sur-base and dado seem at present to be quite out of fashion; nor, indeed, do I think it very desirable that they should be again received into favor. It is my opinion, that a room finished with a base only, presents a more chaste and pleasing appearance than when encumbered with a dado and sur-base. When plastering is substituted for the boards of the dado, it is less expensive, and a greater preventive against the cold air.

BASE MOULDINGS.

PLATES XLI. XLII. XLIII. and XLIV.

On these plates are nineteen designs for base mouldings, all of which are drawn in full size for practice. As a very good fashion seems now to prevail, of not using either dados or sur-bases, it is necessary to make the base somewhat larger than it was when these were in fashion. It will be proper to make the plinth to these designs for base mouldings about seven inches wide; in small, low rooms, their size may be somewhat reduced. Correct or incorrect judgment, in considering the size and situation of the room, when base mouldings are to be used, will always have a decided effect on their good or bad appearance.

ARCHITRAVES.

PLATES XLV. XLVI. and XLVII.

THESE plates contain designs for architraves. They are all drawn at full size for practice; but as it is not probable that they will suit every situation, I shall give some general rules for their proportion. Doors and windows in the same room are necessarily of different heights and widths, the windows always being considerably larger than the doors; but it would be highly improper to make two widths of architraves. It therefore becomes necessary to make a compromise between them. I have in practice generally divided the width of the door into six equal parts, and given one to the width of the architrave: say, if the door is three feet wide, one sixth would be six inches, which would be rather too wide for the door; but as the windows in the same room would be from ten to twelve inches wider than the door, six inches would be rather too narrow for the window, if its size only was to be considered; I therefore should make the architrave one sixth of the width of the door.

PLATE XLVIII.

Shows the manner of applying the plinth under the architrave to doors and windows, and also the application of the block at the upper angles of the door or window against which the architrave butts.

D is a section of the block and architrave, and shows clearly how far the block projects front of the architrave.

E is a section of the plinth and architrave, and shows how far the plinth projects front of the architrave.

ARCHITRAVES.

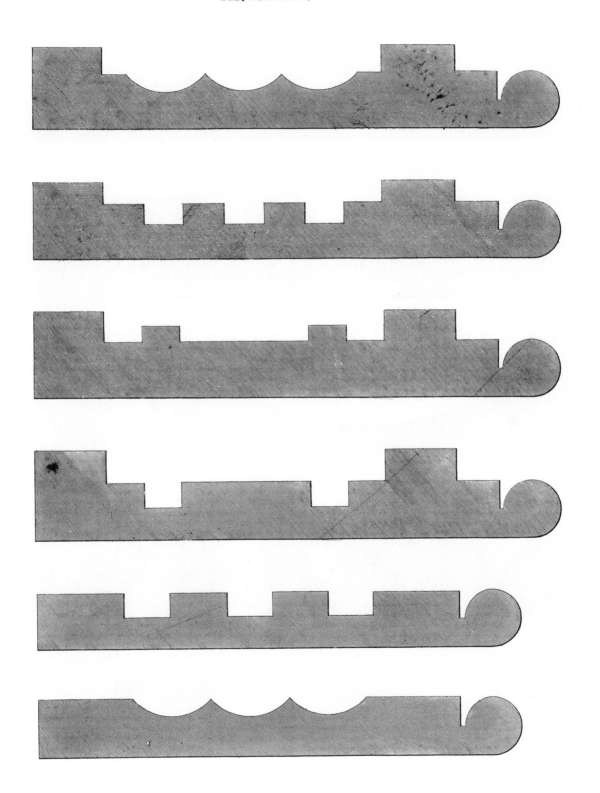

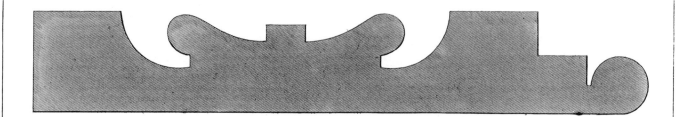

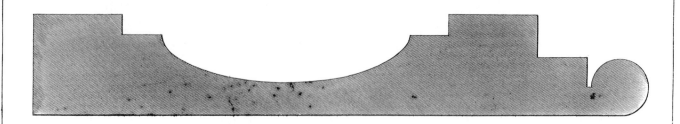

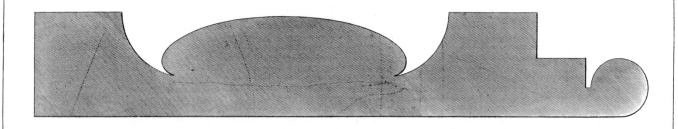

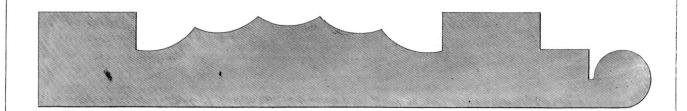

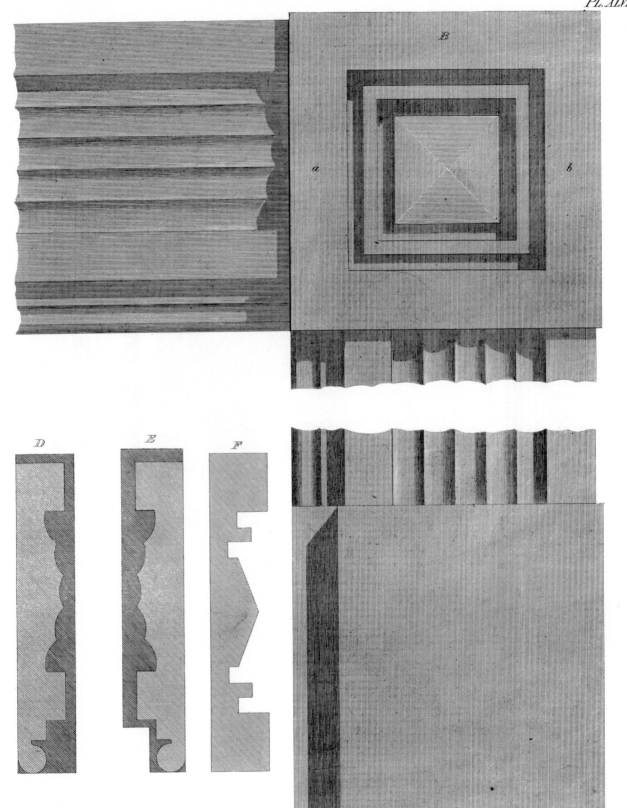

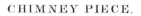

Pilaster ¼ full size.

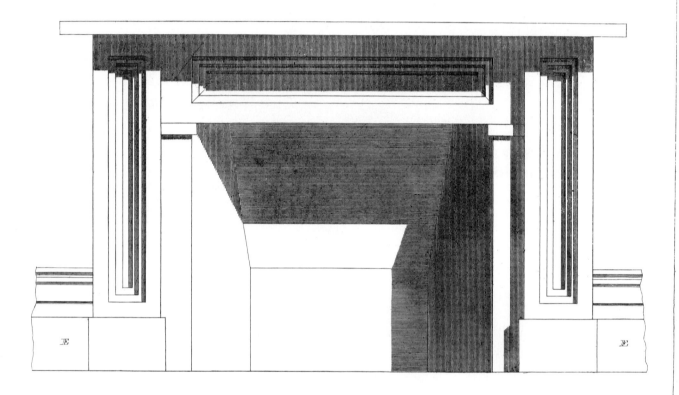

E

E

Scale of feet & inches

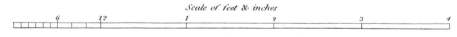

| 6 | 12 | 1 | 2 | 3 | 4 |

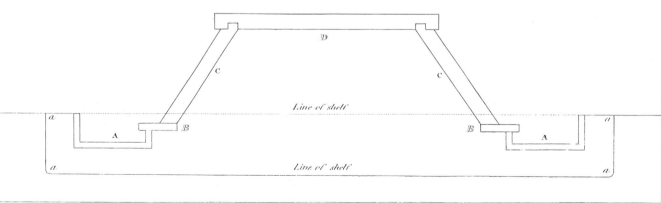

D

C

C

Line of shelf

a

a

A

B

B

A

a

a

Line of shelf

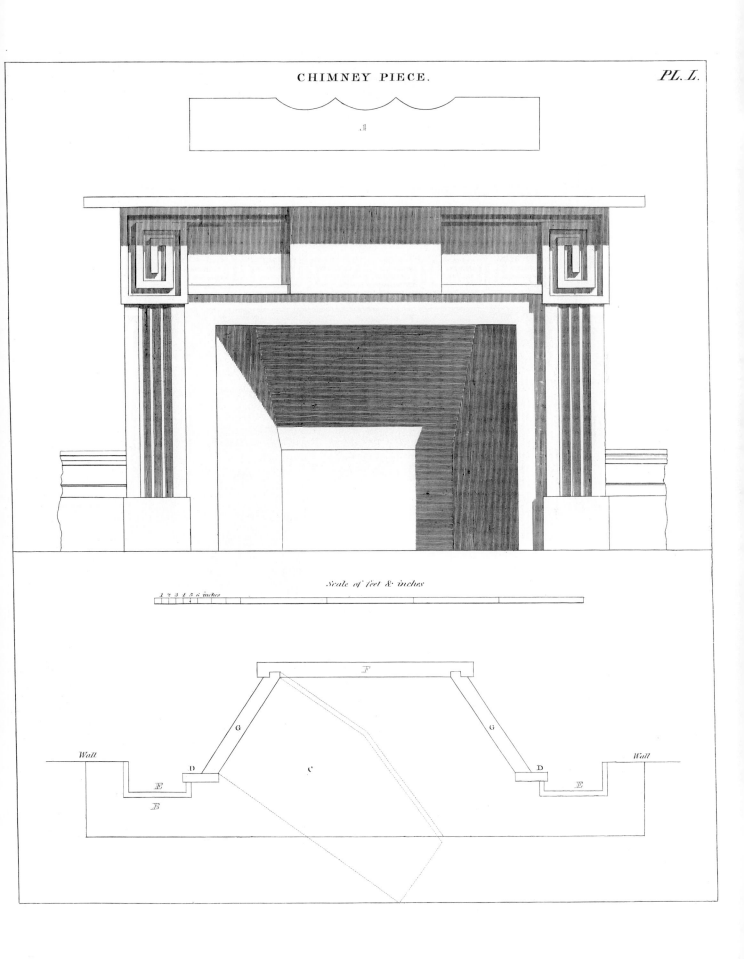

Scale of feet & inches

1 2 3 4 5 6 inches

Section of facing full size

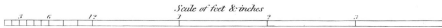

Scale of feet & inches

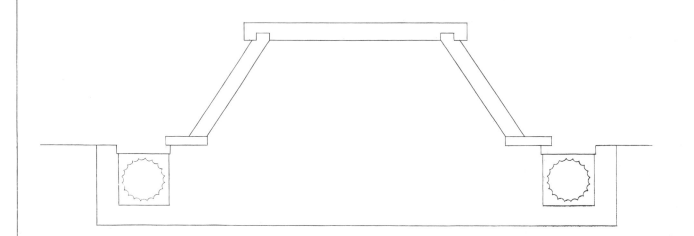

F is a section from *a* to *b* through the block, showing the formation of the panel. It is both proper and common to ornament these panels with rosettes, from the plainest kind up to the most rich and beautiful; and where the panel is large, it may be enriched with the honeysuckle, or any other appropriate ornament.

All the figures on this plate are drawn at half the full size.

CHIMNEY PIECES.

PLATES XLIX. L. and LI.

On these plates are three designs for chimney pieces. These designs are formed suitably for marble, but may be constructed of wood.

In the decoration of chimney pieces, the wildest fancy has been indulged. Their composition should conform to the style and character of the room in which they are placed, whether of marble or of wood. If of wood, they may be painted black and varnished, which will give them a neat appearance, and render them less liable to be soiled with smoke than when painted a light color.

A A on Plate **XLIX.** shows the plan of the pilasters; **C C**, a section of the jambs; and **D**, the section of the back. The jambs and back are intended to be made of soap stone, but may be made of any other kind of stone which will stand the heat of the fire, or of iron. *a a a a* represents the front edge of the cornice, or shelf. **E E** shows how the plinth of the pilasters, and that of the room, should be connected with each other.

On Plate **L.** is shown the plan of the fire place, **E E** being the plan of the pilasters, **G G** that of the jambs, **F** the back, and **D D** the facings. **C** shows an elevation of one of the jambs, with the top end narrowed off to its proper width. Every part of these designs can be accurately measured by the scale of feet and inches annexed to each plate.

Open fire places for burning wood ought to be proportioned, in some degree, to the room in which they are placed. It is, however, difficult to lay down any precise rule for their proportion. An open fire place cannot be made much less than three feet in breadth, if the room be not more than twelve feet square, and should never exceed three feet nine inches in any room, whatever be its size. A fire place of three feet opening between the jambs should have an opening from the hearth upwards of about two feet seven inches.

Where open fire places are made for burning coals, the grate set in them should be about one inch in length for every foot in the length of the room; that is to say, if the room is twenty feet square, make the grate twenty inches long, and about ten inches deep. The top bar of the grate should not be less than eighteen inches, nor more than twenty-four, from the hearth.

GUILOCHE AND FRETS.

PLATE LII.

On this plate are given seven various ornamental pieces of the guiloche and fret, intended for friezes, bands, panels, and various other decorations, the use of which, if tastefully employed,

PL. LII.

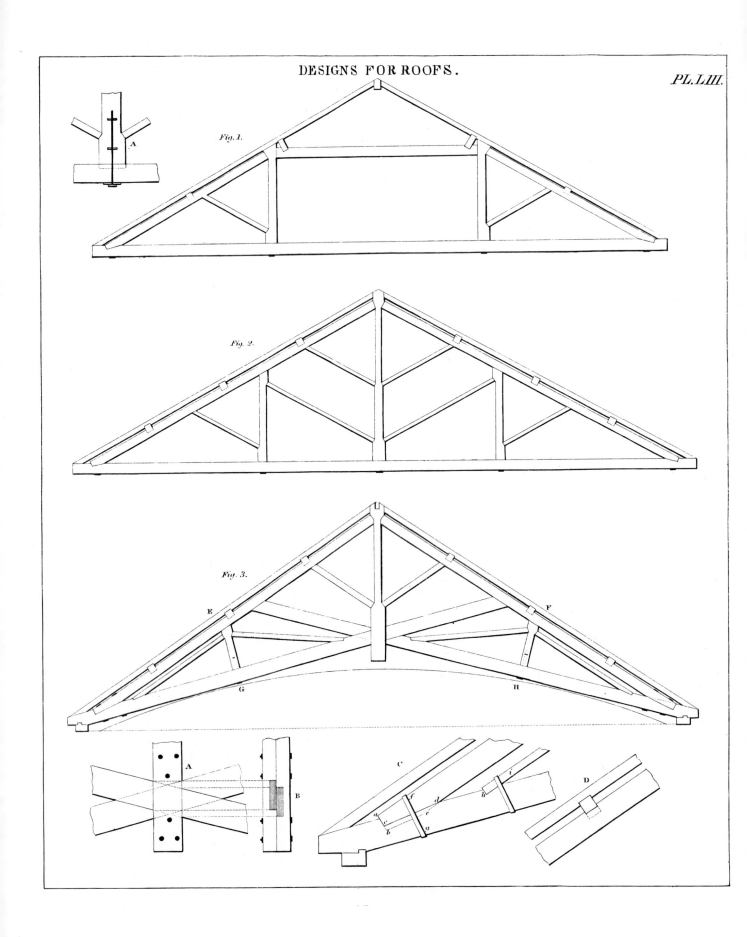

DESIGNS FOR ROOFS.

PL. LIII.

Fig. 1.

Fig. 2.

Fig. 3.

will not fail to produce a chaste and pleasing effect. They lay claim to the highest antiquity, having been used by the Chinese in their earliest periods, from whom they were carried into Egypt, and from thence into Greece, embellishing their buildings as well as their vases. From the nature of their construction, an endless variety of forms may be obtained.

A is composed of parallel right lines, which form geometrical squares of any magnitude, connected together by quadrants of a circle on the outsides. The proportions of the parts to each other are figured on the plate. Fig. B, C and D are composed of circles, as is evident from inspection, and their relative proportions are figured on the plate. E, F and G are three different designs for frets, with their divisions marked on the plate.

CARPENTRY.

PLATE LIII.

On fig. 1 is shown a design for a roof, suitably constructed to cover a dwelling house, where it is desired to use the space between the rafters for lodging rooms. The height of the pitch is equal to two sevenths of the base line of the roof. This is a good pitch for either slates or shingles. The span of this example is calculated for forty-four feet, but it may be extended to fifty or more by proportionally enlarging the size of the timbers of which it is composed.

A shows the method of confining the king post to the tie beams by bolts. In this example, the bolt should be about one inch in diameter, with a strong head of about one and three fourths of an inch in diameter; and a plate of iron about one fourth of an inch thick and of about four by five inches surface, should be placed between the tie beam and the head of the bolt. The nut, which is let into the king post, should be three fourths of an inch thick, and about three inches square. One nut will be sufficient here, but when the strain is very great, two will be required.

The tenon, connecting the king post with the tie beam, is not required to be more than two inches long. The size of the timbers of this example may be as follows: tie beam, seven by twelve inches; principal rafters seven by ten at foot, and seven by eight at head; queen posts, seven by ten; straining beam, seven by eleven; purloins, eight by nine; small rafters, two and three fourths by five; ridge pole, four by seven; braces, four by seven inches.

Fig. 2 shows a design for a trussed roof, which is of the same pitch as that of fig. 1, and is calculated for a span of seventy feet. The construction of this roof is very ancient, strong and simple; it has been executed with great success for churches, theatres, and other large buildings, and is the least expensive and the best constructed plan of any now in use. Size of timbers is as follows: tie beams, eight by twelve; principal rafters, eight by ten at foot, and eight inches square at the head; king posts, eight by twelve; queen posts, eight by ten; purloins, eight by nine; small rafters, two and three fourths by five; braces, three by seven; plates, six by ten inches.

Fig. 3 is a design of a roof for a church, or any other large building, in which it is desired to raise a circular ceiling. It is drawn from a scale of ten feet to one inch, and is calculated for seventy feet span. The perpendicular height of the ridge is equal to one third of the base line of the roof. It will be unsafe to lower the ridge when the recess up into the roof is as great as in this example.

A shows a longitudinal section of the tie beams and king post. The tie beams are locked into each other, so that the outsides of each are in the same plane. The king post is to be made in two parts, and a space cut away in each half, as shown in **B**, so as just to admit the tie beams, when locked together, to pass through them. In this kind of roof, the strain on the tie beam is very great; it will therefore be necessary to make them eight by fifteen inches, and each half of the king post eight by fourteen inches, so that when they are bolted together, the king post will be fourteen inches wide and sixteen inches thick. It will then admit the tie beam to pass through it, and leave four by fourteen inches of solid wood on each side. Diminish it in thickness and in straight lines from the foot of the braces upwards to the head and thickness of the principal rafters.

C shows the method of connecting the tie beam and that of the principal rafter. The joint at the foot of the rafter should be made at right angles with its back, or upper edge. Make $a\ c$ six inches, cutting five and a half of them out of the tie beam. Make the joint $c\ d$ as here represented, and make a tenon to the rafter two inches thick and two and a half long, as shown by the dotted line $b\ e$. It being of the utmost importance that those two timbers should be strongly united, I have represented at $g\ f$ an iron strap or hoop, which should be two inches wide and three eighths of an inch thick; and, in addition to this, there should be at least one good strong iron bolt. At $i\ h$ is shown the method of connecting the trusses for the support of the vertical strain on the rafters, at **F** and **E**. The foot of this truss must also be cut at right angles with its upper edge, and let into the tie beam about two and three fourths of an inch, and must be confined to it by an iron hoop one and a half inch wide and three eighths of an inch thick. A bolt will be necessary at both **G** and **H**.

D shows the method of fitting the purloins to both the principal and common rafters. The top of the principal rafter is to be notched one inch only, in order to receive the purloin; and the purloin is to be notched, so as to be left four inches above the principal rafter. Notch the common rafters on the under side about two inches.

The sizes of the tie beams, principal rafters, and king posts, have already been given. Make the purloins eight by ten; the king posts, **E** and **F**, each eight by ten; the braces three by eight; the small rafters two and three fourths by six; and the plates seven by twelve inches. The principal rafters should not be more than nine feet from centre to centre.

PLATE LIV.

To find the Length and Backing of Hip Rafters.

Let **A B C D** be the plan of the building and the angles of the roof; draw **E A, E B, E C** and **E D**, the base lines, over which the hip rafters are to stand; let *b n m* be the pitch of the roof; draw **E F** at right angles with **E A**, and equal to *o n*, the pitch of the roof; then draw **A F**, which is the length of the hip rafter; draw *g k h* at any distance from the angle **A**, and at right angles with **A E**; make *k i* equal to *k r*, or from *k* to the nearest point of the top line of the hip rafter, draw *g i* and *i h*, the backing of the hip rafter required. This method will give the backing of the hip rafter, whether the building be square or bevelling.

Fig. 2 is the plan of an octagon dome, *a b* being the base line of the given rib. No. 2 shows the curve of the dome, which in this case

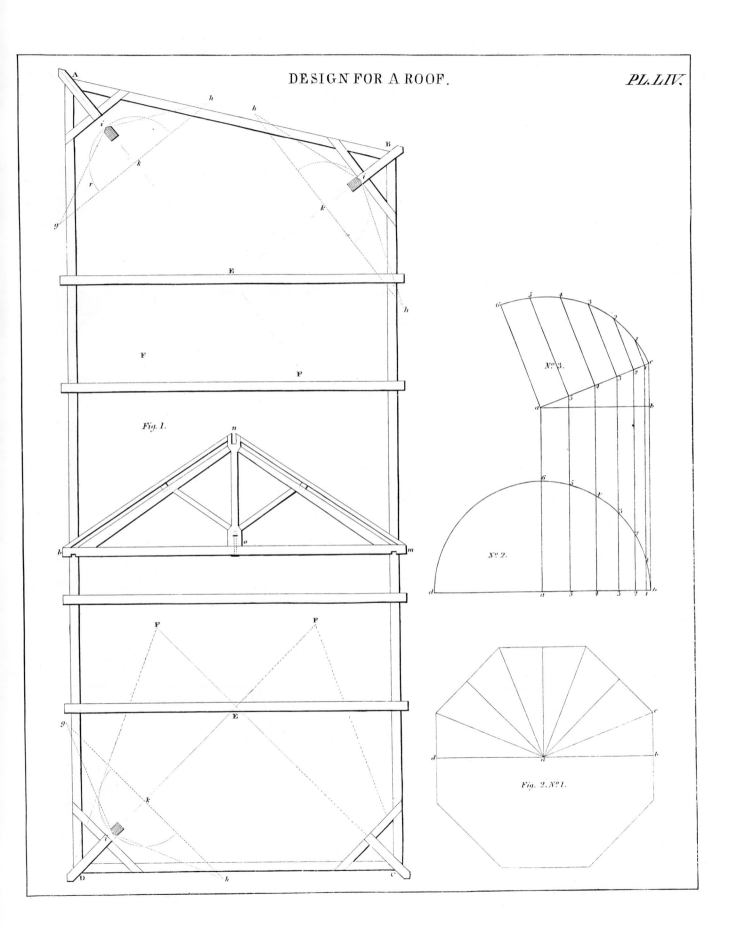

Fig. 1.

Nº 3.

Nº 2.

Fig. 2. Nº 1.

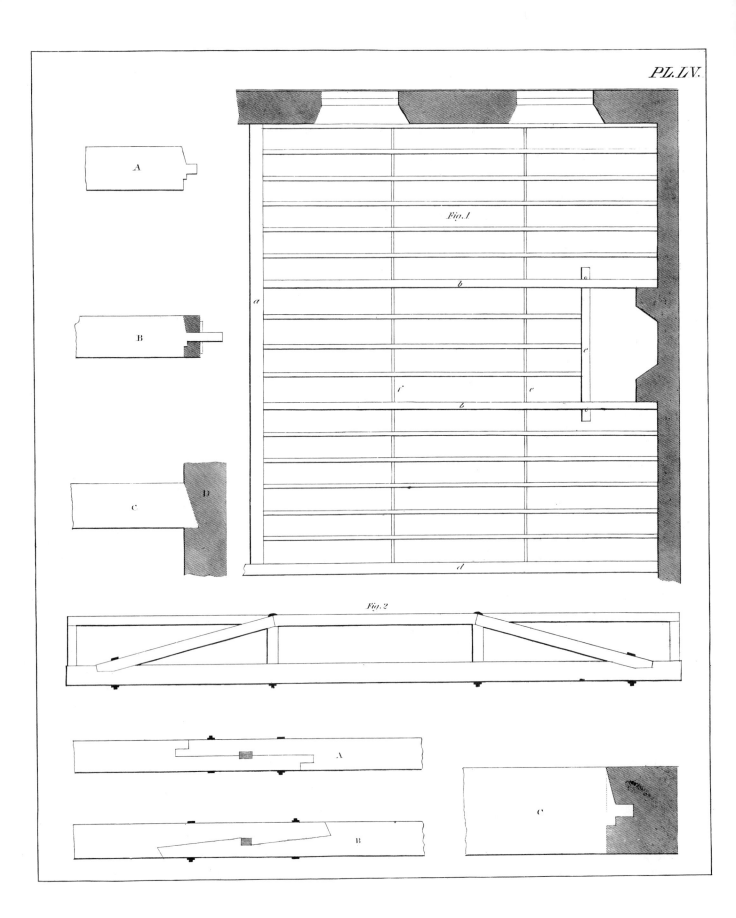

Fig.1

Fig.2

is half of a circle drawn from the centre *a*. Draw *a* 6, cutting the circle at 6, and at right angles with *d b*, and produce it to *a ;* divide *b* 6 into six or more equal parts. Make *a b* No. 3 parallel and equal to *a b* No. 2, *b c* equal to *b c* No. 1, and join *c a*. Then draw ordinates from *a b* No. 2 to *a c* No. 3, parallel to *a* 6, cutting the circle in No. 2 at the points 1, 2, 3, 4, 5, and *a c* No. 3 at 1, 2, 3, 4, 5. Draw *a* 6 at right angles with *a c*, also 5 5, 4 4, 3 3, 2 2, and 1 1, parallel to *a* 6, and equal to 1 1, 2 2, 3 3, 4 4, 5 5 and *a* 6 in No. 2, and then trace the curve *c* 1 2 3 4 5 and 6, which will, when placed in its right position, correspond with the given circle.

PLATE LV.

Fig. 1 shows the method of framing floors with plank, or wide joists. In this example, the joists are eighteen feet long ; for that bearing the common joists should be twelve by two and a quarter inches, and the trimmer joists, *b b* and *c*, twelve by four and a half inches. They should be got out by a mould, made about three quarters of an inch crowning. The girders, *a* and *d*, should each be twelve inches deep and seven inches thick. A shows the method of making the tenons to the common joists, and B those of the trimmer joists. B also shows a section of the trimmer when the mortise is made through it. D shows the section of a brick wall, and C the shape of the ends of the joists when they lie on the wall. *f* and *e* show two courses of bridging. Great care is necessary in fitting them between the joists ; they ought not to be driven in so hard as to crowd either the wall or girders out of their places, nor ought they to be too loose. They may be made of boards, but they should be as wide as the joists, and the ends cut so as to fit the sides of the joists in the most perfect manner. The expense of this kind of floor is about one third less than that of any other kind, and it certainly is more equal in its strength than is the timber and joist floor. When a good ceiling is required, and the joists are over fifteen feet in length, it is advisable to fur them with strips of boards of two and a half or three inches wide. It appears, by an experiment made by Professor Robinson, that the saving of timber is considerably more than one third. The experiment is thus related: Two models were made of eighteen inches square, one framed with girders, binding, bridging and ceiling joists, and the other with single joists, containing the same quantity of timber as the girders alone of the framed floor. They were both put into wooden trunks, of eighteen inches square, resting on projections within the trunks. Small shot were gradually poured over each; the framed floor broke down with three hundred and twenty-seven pounds, and the single joisted floor with four hundred and eighty-seven pounds.

Fig. 2 is a design for a truss, proper for the support of the front of a gallery in a church, or any other place where the bearing required is so large that a single timber is not sufficient to support the weight which is to be placed thereon. A and B show two different methods for scarfing timbers, and C represents a mortise and tenon proper for connecting large timbers; the thickness of the tenon may generally be about one sixth of the whole depth of the timber on which it is made.

PLATE LVI.

Fig. 1 is an elevation of a trussed partition, in which it is convenient to place two door ways; and in that case it becomes necessary to place the truss over the doors. The tie beam and king posts are locked into each other at *a a*.

At fig. 2 is shown the best methods of framing the head of a principal rafter, and also of the braces to the king posts. It is preferable, where it can conveniently be done, to make the joints of both at right angles with their working sides, like *a* and *c*; but where that cannot be done, the next best method is shown at *d b*. **A** represents a side view of the tie beam, and **B** a section of the plate, and also the best method of cogging them together.

Fig. 3 shows how to draw the different angle brackets, to form a cove ceiling; and by the same principles the different curvatures for the ribs of a dome, or any other circular roof, may be drawn. Let *a b* 10 and *c* represent the angles of a room over which it is desired to make a groin ceiling; on the line *c* 10 on 5, and with the distance 5 *c* or 5 10, describe the half or given circle; draw the diagonal line *c b*; divide the circle **A**, from *c* around to 10, into any number of parts, as here into ten; draw lines from each of these divisions, and parallel to *c a*, cutting *c* 10 and *c b* each at 1, 2, 3, 4, 5, 6, 7, 8 and 9, and from those points on *c b* draw lines at right angles from *c b*, and also from the same points draw lines through 10 *b*, and at right angles with 10 *b*; make the distance 1 1, 2 2, 3 3, 4 4, 5 5, &c. in both **C** and **B**, exactly equal to the corresponding distance 1 1, 2 2, 3 3, 4 4, 5 5, &c. in **A**, and through those points trace the curves in both **C** and **B**, which gives the bracket required.

Fig. 4 shows how to draw the different curvatures of the edges of boards for the covering of a dome. Draw the vertical line 8 *g*, and divide one half of the dome into as many parts as there are intended to be courses of boards, as in this example into seven;

through 1 and 2 draw a right line, cutting 8 *g* at *j*, and on *j* as a centre, with the distances *j* 1 and *j* 2, describe both edges of the board *i*, and through 2 and 3 draw a right line, cutting 8 *g* at *k* ; on *k*, and with the distances *k* 2 and *k* 3, describe both edges of the board *h*. Proceed in the same manner until the boards *g, f, e* and *d* are completed.

General Observations on Carpentry.

The floors in a room of eighteen or twenty feet square should be made crowning, about three fourths of an inch, and in the same proportion if the room is larger. The curve should be that of a segment of a circle, and rise equally from each side of the room to the centre. Under doors, the floor should be raised a little, so that the door may swing freely over it, without touching. Where this precaution is not attended to, and the floor made straight, it will, by its own weight and that put upon it, soon settle below a straight line, and, of course, crack the plastering beneath it. It will be wise to observe the same precaution in all horizontal and inclined framings of any considerable bearing.

It is recommended, in many practical books on carpentry, to make the mortises in girders, beams and other large timbers, near the upper side of the stick : the reason given for this is, that when the girder settles, it tends to compress that part above the middle in the direction of its length, and proportionably to lengthen the part below the centre ; and that, if the tenon be inserted near the upper edge, the compression of the girder will press hard on each side of the tenon, and thus prevent the girder from being weakened by the mortise. But it is evident, that if the tenon be of any tolerable width, its shrinkage will be greater than the compression, and that no advantage, therefore, can be gained by the above method. As the centre of the girder is less affected by either the compression above the middle, or the expansion below it, the middle is the best place for the mortise, which may generally be made about one sixth part of the depth of the girder. Great care is required, in making mortises and tenons, that they may fit each other exactly. The same care is also required in making all kinds of joints, so that the part out of sight may fit as completely as that which is seen. Double tenons in house-framing are not admissible. I know of no advantage gained by them, but, on the contrary, they cut up the girder too much, and are not often brought up to so good a joint as single ones; nor does the pin have the effect to draw up the joint; for it generally cripples before it passes through the lower tenon.

Joists in framed floors, purloins, common rafters, &c., will gain much additional strength by being notched into their supports, and made in continued lengths. In the framing of roofs, where bearing timbers are not at right angles with each other, the joints should be made a little open at the angular points, as there will always be a shrinkage of the timber, which will cause a small settlement of the roof; and the joints, being likewise made to bear on their angular points, will either be crippled, or indented by the strain, and thereby, unless the above precaution is taken, cause a further settlement.

All bolts, nuts, straps, and plates of iron, when used either in damp situations or on green timber, should be well secured against rust; since, after the rust has once fastened upon them, (and this usually happens very soon, unless provided against,) it will continue to eat into the iron until its strength is destroyed. Mr. Sweaton recommends, as a preventive against rust, to heat the iron to about a blue heat, and immediately strike over its surface with raw linseed oil, which will fill up the pores of the iron, and effectually protect it against corrosion.

In the directions given for the size of the timbers in the foregoing examples for roofs, I have supposed them to be of white pine : but if they should be made of hard pine, the sizes may be somewhat reduced ; or, if of oak, a considerable reduction may be made. It is best to use hard wood for the king posts, and particularly when the roof is of large dimensions ; for the tendency of the strain is to draw the king post in the direction of its length, and that of the principal rafters to compress them in the direction of their length. A great pressure is therefore sustained between the head of the king post and that of the principal rafters, which will cause the heads of the rafters to indent themselves into the head of the king post, and thereby cause a small settlement of the roof. The king post ought to be well seasoned, and its breadth no more than is required for its connexion with the head of the rafters, and the support of the strain necessarily thrown upon it by the weight of the roof; for a shrinkage in its breadth would cause a small settlement of the roof.

HANDRAILING.

PLATE LVII.

DESIGNS FOR HANDRAILS AND NEWELLS.

FIG. 1 is a design for a stair post or newell, which is drawn at full size. Fig. 2, 3 and 4 are sections of stair rails, which are also drawn at full size for practice. It has been customary to lay down rules for drawing sections of handrails composed of parts of circles and straight lines; but they certainly are not so graceful as those here laid down, which are composed of parts of ellipses and straight lines.

PLATE LVIII.

To draw the Scroll for a Handrail. Divide *a b*, the width of the scroll, into nine equal parts; make *b c* and *a d* each equal to one of these parts, and at right angles with *a b*; draw *d c*; join *c b* and *d a*; also join the diagonal line *c a*. Draw *f e* perpendicular to *a b*, and at a distance from *c* of five of the nine parts into which *a b* is divided. Divide *f g* into two equal parts at *h*, on *h*, with the distance *h f* or *h g*. Draw the half circle *f o g* (see fig. 2, on which the centres are drawn on a large scale) from *f*, and through *o* draw the diagonal *f o i*; also from *g* draw *g o k*, cutting *o* exactly where the half circle *f o g* intersects the diagonal *c a*; then draw *g i, i k, k l, l m, m n, n p, p q*, &c., at right angles with each other, cutting the diagonals at *g i, i k, k l, l m, m n, n p, p q*, &c. Then, with the distance *f c*, and on *f*, draw the quarter of a circle *c e*; on *g*, and

with the distance *g e*, draw *e a ;* on *i*, and with the distance *i a*,
draw *a r ;* and so on, until you have completed the outside circle,
drawing one quarter of the circle from each centre. The inside
circle is drawn from the same centres as the outside.

v v show where to place the face of the two first risers. The
dotted line, *e a d r l s*, represents the extreme projection of the
nosing around the curtail step, and *z z* the extreme projection of the
nosing to the second step. The lines *w x*, which are drawn from the
same centres as the rail, show where to place the balusters.

Fig. 3 represents the method of making the curtail step ; *a a a*
represents the riser glued on to the block ; *b b*, keys for keying up
the riser around the curtail step, when glued on ; *c*, a block to be
glued on to both riser and step, for the purpose of keeping them firm
in their place.

*To draw the Face Mould, for Squaring the twisted part of
the Scroll.* Fig. 4 is a plan of the rail, in all respects like fig. 1.
a b c No. 2 is the pitch board, No. 3 the face mould. Draw *d h*
through the centre of the scroll, and parallel to *a b ;* draw *a d* at
right angles with *a b*, and *h h h* at right angles with *a b*, cutting
the upper edge of the pitch board at *h ;* draw *h h* No. 3 at right
angles with *a c*, the upper edge of the pitch board, and *a d* also at
right angles with *a c*. Make *a d* and *h h* No. 3 each equal to *a d*
and *h h* No. 1 ; join *d h* No. 3. Draw ordinates through No. 1 at
e e e, f f f, and *g g g*, cutting the upper edge of the pitch board at
e f g, and from these points draw ordinates at right angles with *a c*
across the face mould, cutting *d h* at *e f g*. Then, on the scroll No.
1, divide *d e, f g* and *g h* each into any number of parts, either equal
or unequal ; draw ordinates through each one of these divisions, 1 2 3,

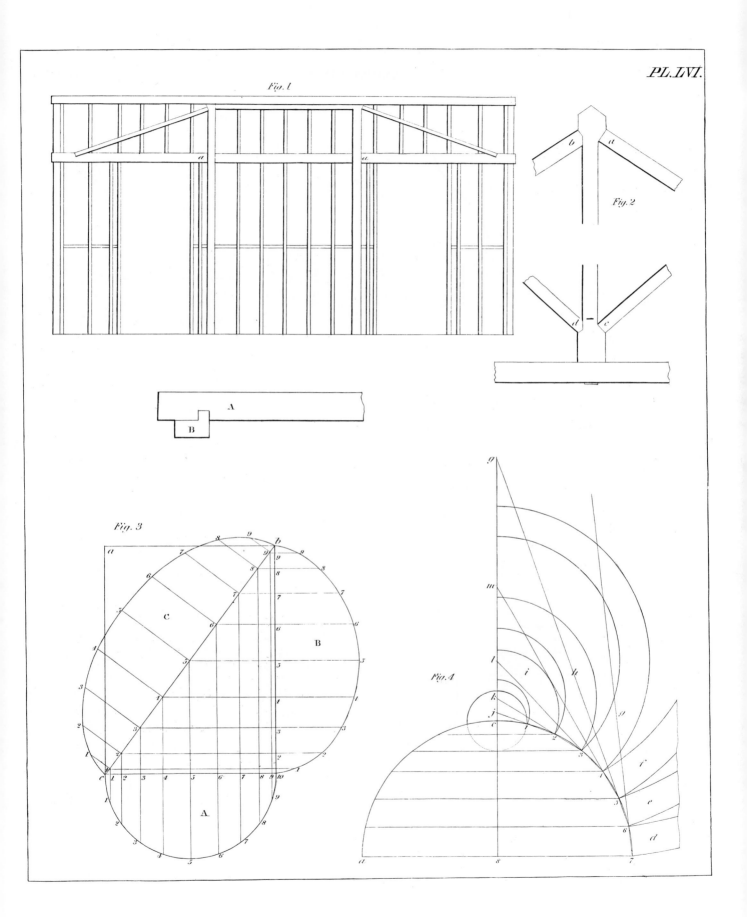

Fig. 1

Fig. 2

A

B

Fig. 3

Fig. 4

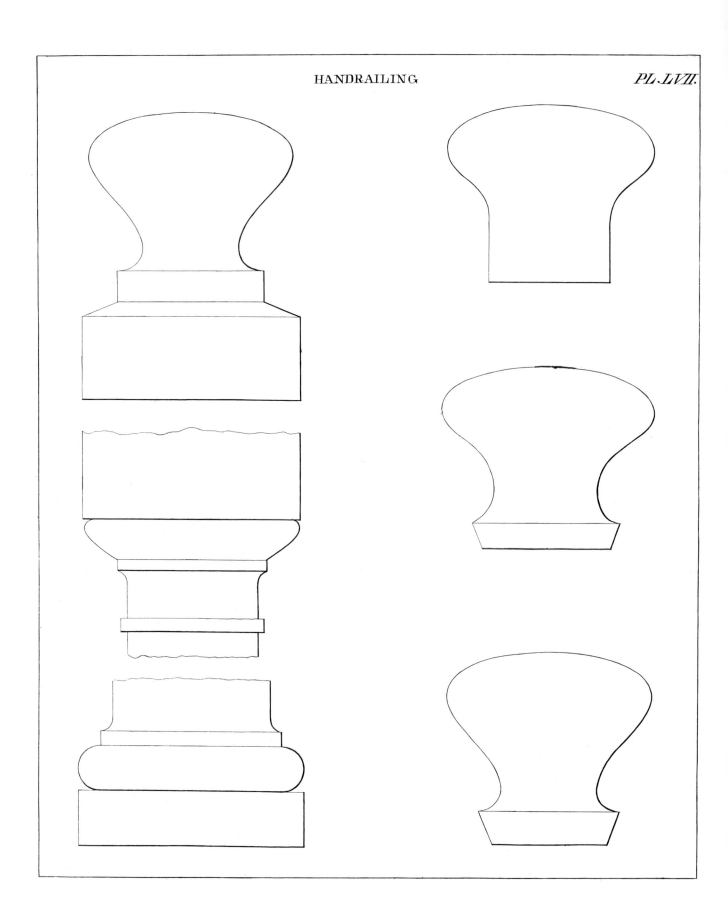

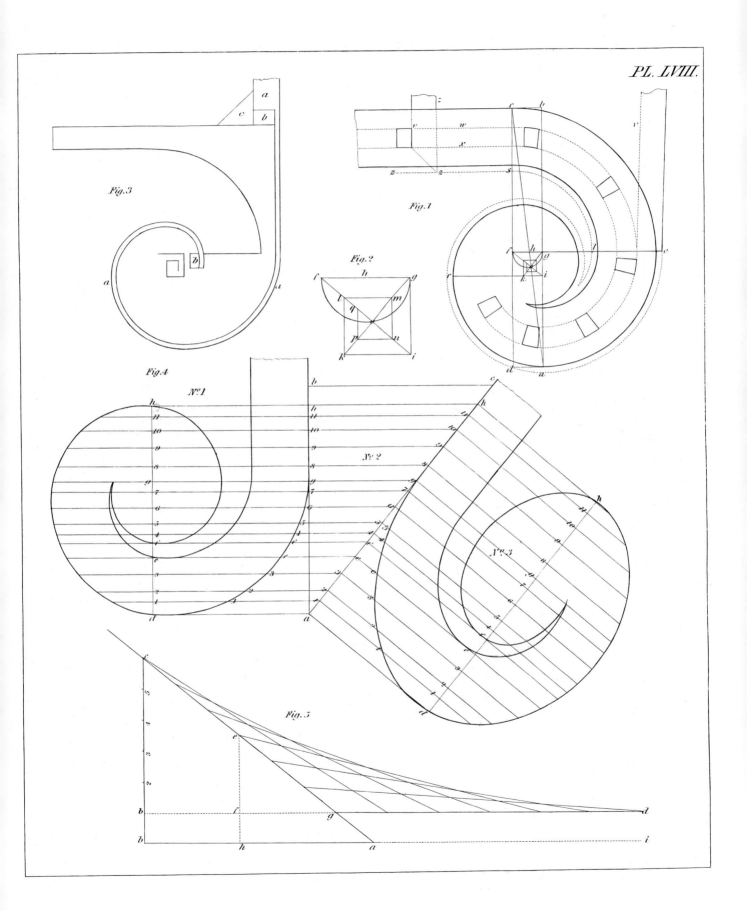

PL. LVIII.

Fig.3

Fig.1

Fig.2

Fig.4

N.º1

N.º2

N.º3

Fig.5

Fig. 1

Fig. 2

Fig. 3

Fig. 4

4 5 6 7, 8 9 10 11, parallel to those before drawn, cutting the upper edge of the pitch board at **1, 2, 3, 4, 5, 6, 7, 8, 9, 10, 11,** and from those points, and at right angles with the upper edge of the pitch board *a c,* draw ordinates across the face mould, cutting *d h* at **1, 2, 3, 4, 5, 6, 7, 8, 9, 10, 11.**

From *d h* No. **1** take the distance **1 1,** and set it off from **1** to **1** on *d h* No. **3**; then take **2 2, 3 3,** *e e,* *f f,* **4 4, 5 5, 6 6,** &c., on No. **1,** and set them off from *d h* No. **3, 2** to **2, 3** to **3,** *e* to *e,* *f* to *f,* **4** to **4, 5** to **5, 6** to **6,** &c. Proceed in the same manner to take from *d h* No. **1** all the distances on both inside and outside of the scroll, and set them off both ways on all the corresponding ordinates from *d h* No. **3**; then trace the curve through all these points, and it will complete the plan of the face mould.

To draw the Falling Mould. Fig. **5,** *a b c,* represents the pitch board. Divide *b c,* its height, into six parts, to give the level of the scroll; the distance *b f* is from the face of the riser to the beginning of the twist, and the distance from *f* to *d* is equal to the stretchout of the scroll, from *c,* the beginning of the twist, to *a,* on fig. **1,** each being any part taken at discretion more than the first quarter of the scroll; divide *e g,* the rake of the pitch board, and *g d,* the level of the rail, each into the same number of equal parts, and, by intersecting lines, complete the top edge of the mould, and make the under edge parallel thereto.

PLATE LIX.

RECIPROCAL SPIRALS AND SCROLLS.

To draw the Reciprocal Spiral and Scroll. Suppose a circle drawn from the centre of the intended spiral, and divided into eight equal parts. Draw lines through the centre of the spiral, cutting each of these eight parts on the supposed circle, of a sufficient length to intersect the curve of the scroll, as represented on fig. 1, at **P, K, L, R, S, T, U, V**; and suppose the length of the ordinate **O P** to be given, make **B A** in fig. 2 equal to **O P** fig. 1, and draw **E D** at any angle from **A B**; the number of revolutions intended to be made in the scroll will determine the number of parts into which **B D** is to be divided. If one revolution is wanted, it will require eight parts; if one and a half, twelve parts; if two, sixteen parts; and so on. Make **E B** and **C A** each equal to **B 1**; from **C** as a centre draw **C 1, C 2, C 3, C 4, &c.**, cutting **B A** at *a, b, c, d, &c.* It has already been mentioned that **B A** is equal to **O P** fig. 1. Make **O K** equal to **A** *a* fig. 2, and **O L** fig. 1 equal to **A** *b* fig. 2; make **O R** fig. 1 equal to **A** *c* fig. 2; also make **O S, O T, O U** and **O V**, in fig. 1, each respectively equal to **A** *d*, **A** *e*, **A** *f*, and **A** *g*, in fig. 2, &c., and draw the curve through **P, K, L, R, S, T, U, V, &c.**, which will be the spiral required. The scroll, fig. 3, is drawn from the scale **F G**, fig. 2, the distance **G J** being equal to that of *o m*, fig. 3; **G F**, fig 2, being equal to *o a*, fig. 3; and the distances *o b, o c, o d* and *o e* are respectively equal to the distances **G 1, G 2, G 3, G 4, &c.** The scroll may be drawn by centres, as follows: with the distance *o a*, and on *f*, draw *k a b;* with the distance *o b*, and on *g*, draw *b c;* with the distance *o c*, and on *h*, draw *c d;* with the distance *o d*, and on *i*, draw *d e, &c.*

It will be perceived that this scroll is not so open as that of fig. 1: the reason is obvious; the lines **A B** and **F G** are not parallel; they make an angle of seventeen degrees, and the divisions on **F G** are much nearer equal than those on **B A**. It is therefore evident, that the nearer equal the divisions are, the closer will be the scroll, as is more plainly shown by the scroll fig. 4, the divisions of which are taken from the scale **H I**, which makes an angle with **A B** of forty-five degrees. As this spiral can easily be made close, or to expand at pleasure, and as its curve is more graceful than any of those which are drawn by centres, it will be found exceedingly useful in stair building, and it can be used with success for many other architectural purposes.

PLATE LX.

TO FIND THE MOULDS FOR MAKING STAIR RAILS ON A SEMICIRCULAR PLAN, WITH EIGHT WINDERS.

To draw the Falling Mould, Fig. 1. First draw the plan of the rail and winders as in fig. 2; then draw the line *d* 8 equal to the height of all the winders, eight in this example; make *d e* and 8 *c* each at right angles with *d* 8, and *d e* equal to the development of **E D**, the quadrantal part of the rail; in fig. 2 also make 8 *c* equal to the development of the quadrantal part of the rail **D 8.** Make *e k* and *h i* each equal to the rise of one step, and parallel to *d* 8; make *k g* equal to the tread of one step, and parallel to *d f.*

In fig. 1 join *g e, e c* and *c i*, which is the central line of the straight part of the rail; then set off on each side about an inch for the depth of the rail, which is generally about two inches, from *e,* the point where you intend to have the straight and curved parts of the rail join, as at *e o* and *e p* (see fig. 8). Divide *e o* and *e p* each into the same number of equal parts, as here into six. Through each of these divisions draw lines intersecting each other, and these lines will produce the curve required for finishing the falling mould.

Produce *d e* in fig. 1 to *f,* and make *e f* equal to the straight part of the rail E F ; draw *f s* at right angles with *d f,* cutting the top of the rail at *s ;* draw *s t* parallel and equal to *f d.* Then make *c l* equal to the straight part of the rail, 8 9, on fig. 2 ; draw *l m* at right angles with 8 *h,* cutting the top of the rail at *m,* and *m n* parallel and equal to 8 *l ;* then join *n* 8 and *s* 4, and *m* will show where the rail is to be joined.

To draw the Face Mould. Take from the plan of the rail on fig. 2, D E B C, the quadrantal part, and E F A B, the straight part, of the rail, and transfer them to fig. 3 No. 2; draw the chord line A C, produced to 1 and 5 ; draw 5 D H 5, C *o u c* and 1 F G, at right angles with the chord line A C, and G H parallel to the chord line A C. Then take the distance from *t* to *u* in fig. 1, and set it from *u* on G H, fig. 3, to *c;* draw G *c* produced to 5 ; then draw from the chord line A C No. 2, 6 J *n t* 6, 4 I *m s* 4, 3 B *l r* 3, 2 *e* E *q* 2 and A *k p a ;* and at right angles with G 5 draw G F, *a k,* 2 E, 3 *l,* 4 *m,* 6 *n, c o* and 5 D. Transfer the distances 5 D in No. 2 to 5 D in No. 1, from C *o* No. 2 to C *o* No. 1, from 6 *n* to 6 *n,* from 4 *m* to 4 *m,* from 3 *l* to 3 *l,* from 2 E to 2 E, from A *k* to *a k,* and from 1 F to G F ; also from 6 J to 6 *j,* from 4 I to 4 *i,* from 3 B to 3 *b,* and from 2 *e* to 2 *e ;* then trace the curves F *k* E *l m n o* D and *c j i b.* The lines *b e a* and F *k* E are straight, and E *b* shows where the straight and circular parts of the rail join.

Fig. 4 shows the face mould for the upper quarter part of the rail, which, I think, will be clearly understood without further explanation. The height of the face mould is taken from *u* to *n* on fig. 1, and applied to *v n* on fig. 4.

Fig. 7 shows the edge of the plank on which the face mould fig. 3 is to be applied; and fig. 6 that on which the face mould fig. 4 is to be applied. The angle *c a b*, in fig. 7, must be exactly equal to the angle H 5 G, in fig. 3, No. 1 ; and the angle *c a b*, in fig. 6, to the angle *v n u*, in fig. 4. The points of the face mould at *c* and *a* must be applied exactly to those at *a* and *c* on the upper side of the plank fig. 7, and also to the points *b* and *d* on the lower side of the plank.

PLATE LXI.

TO FIND THE MOULDS FOR A STAIR RAIL WITH A SEMICIRCLE OF EIGHT WINDERS.

Let fig. 1 be the plan of the rail, on which the risers are marked 1, 2, 3, *a*, 5, 6, 7, 8, and let A D E H T I No. 2 be the quadrantal part of the rail, and exactly equal to *e a h i* in fig. 1 ; and let E F G H, the straight part of the rail in fig. 3 No. 2, be equal to *e f g h* in fig. 1, I being the upper and F the lower resting points ; make D, the middle resting point, equal to one half of the stretch-out of the rail from A to F, and draw I D. In the figure of the falling mould, which has been described in page 91, set up on the line *a b* the height of each of the eight risers; draw *a e* at right angles with *a b*, and equal to the stretchout of the rail from A to E. Produce *a e* to *f*, and make *e f* equal to E F, the straight part of the rail. Draw *f l* parallel to *a b*, cutting the top of the falling mould at *l ;* draw *l i* parallel and equal to *f a ;* make *i d* equal to the development of **A D**, and *e f* equal to **E F**. On *a f* make *a d* equal to **I D** ; draw *d m* parallel to *a b*, cutting the upper side of the falling mould at *m*, and draw *m n* at right angles with *a b*, cutting *a b* at *n*. Draw *d r* parallel to *a b*, cutting *m n* at *r*, and from the point *o*, on the upper side of the falling mould, and through *r*, draw *o q*, cutting *l i* at *q ;* make **I Q** equal to *i q ;* then draw **Q F**, touching the point of the rail at **F**, and produce it to **K** ; draw **K L** at right angles with **Q K**, and **B I Z Z** parallel to **Q K** ; make **Z Z** equal to *i o* in fig. 2. Draw **K Z**, and produce it to **L**, and draw **A L L** ; also draw other ordinates from the outside of the rail, cutting **K L** at **Y** *b*, *c*, **U**, **G**, and from these points, and also from **L**, **Z** and **K**, draw ordinates at right angles with **K L**, cutting the convex side of the face mould at **A**, **B**, **C**, *b*, *c*, *o*, *e*, **E**, **F** ; then find the points on the concave side of the face mould, and trace the curves as directed in page 92.

How to apply the Face Mould on each Side of the Plank, so that, when the Wood is cut away, the Curved Surfaces may stand perpendicular to the Plan. In fig. 5, let *a b c d e f g* be the figure of the face mould, placed in the proper position to the pitch line *g i*. In fig. 6, let **Y** represent the edge, **X** the upper side, and **Z** the under side of the plank from which the rail is to be made ; make the angle *g* **K L** equal to the angle **L L K**. In fig. 3, place the points of the face mould at *g* and *i* on **X**, and mark off the plank by the edges of the mould. Draw **L** *g* at right angles with the arris of the plank *g i ;* then make the angle **L** *g* **K** on **Z** equal to the angle *g e i* fig. 5. And in fig. 6 make **L** *g* equal to *g* **K** ; draw *g e* parallel to the lower arris of the plank, and place the points of the face mould at *g* and *e*, and mark by both of its edges.

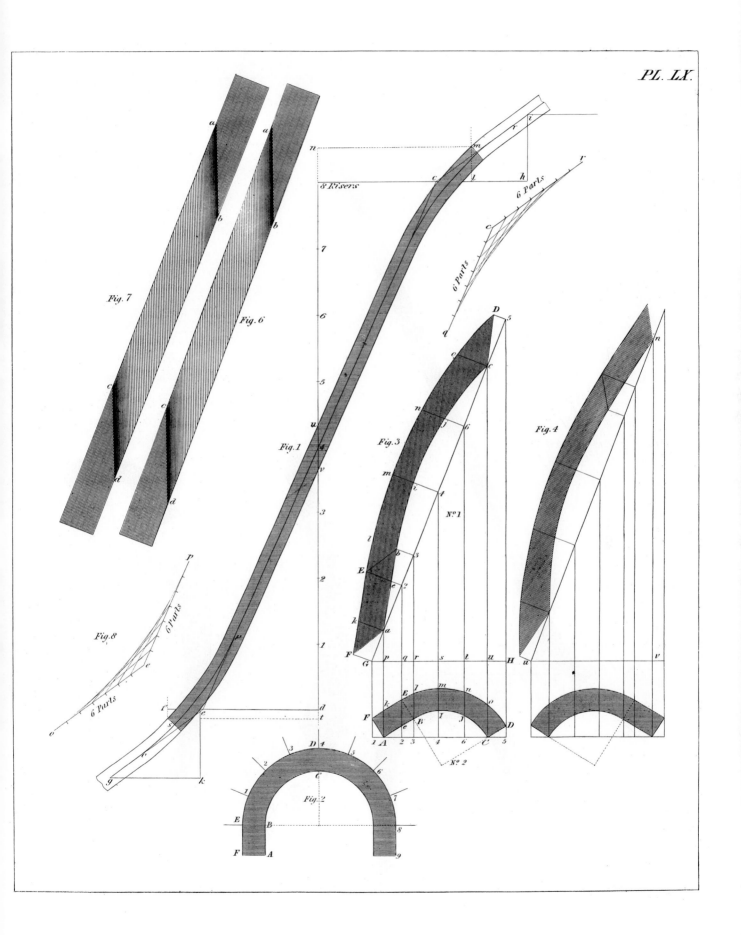

PL. LX.

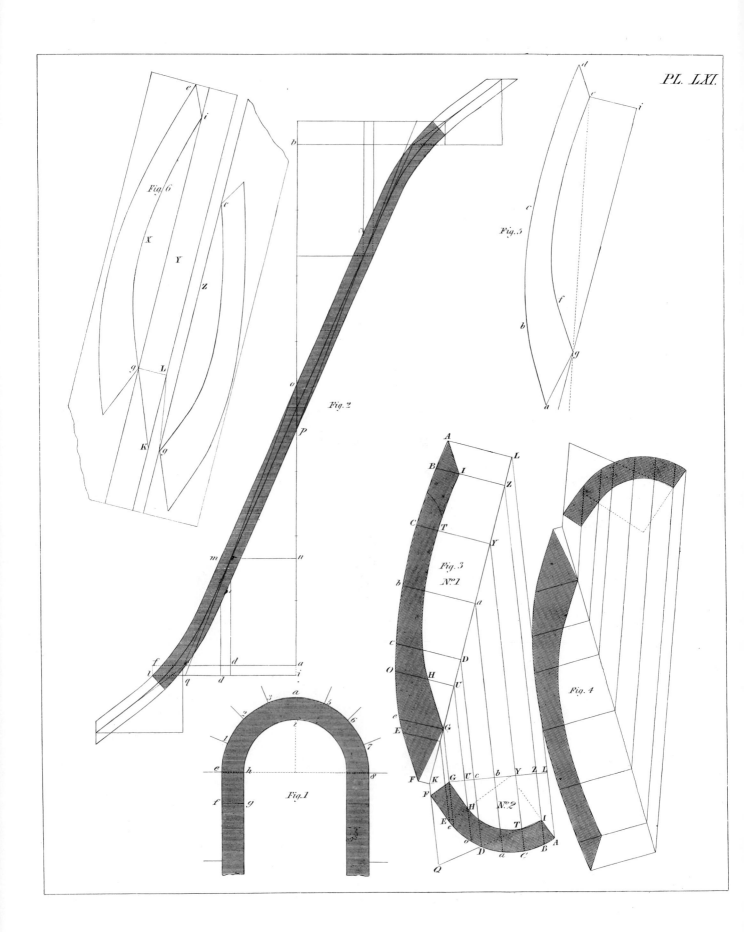

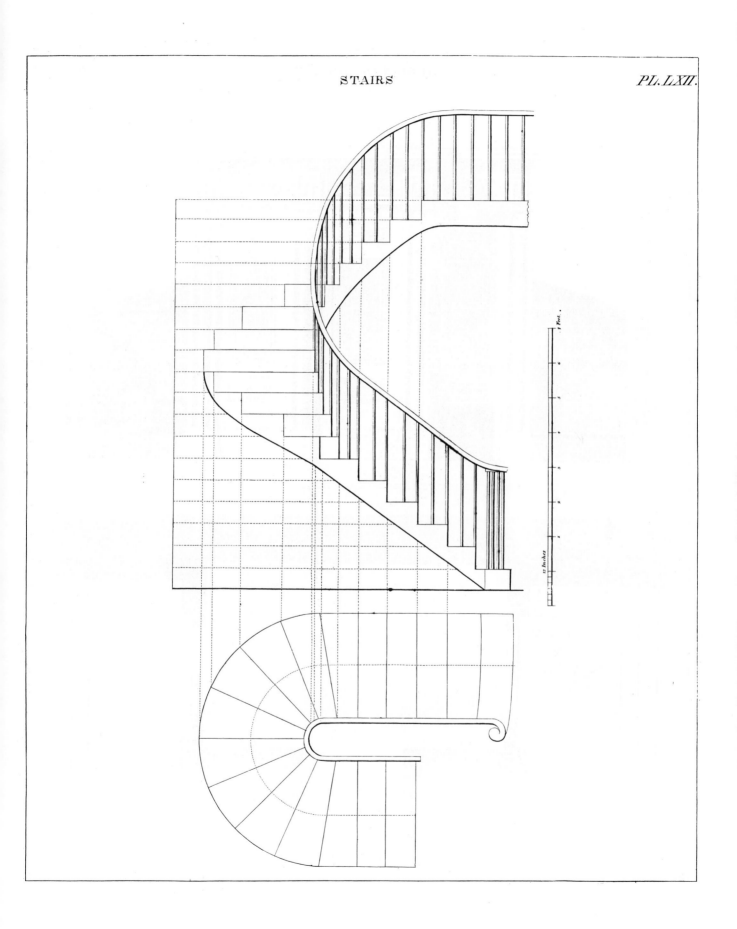

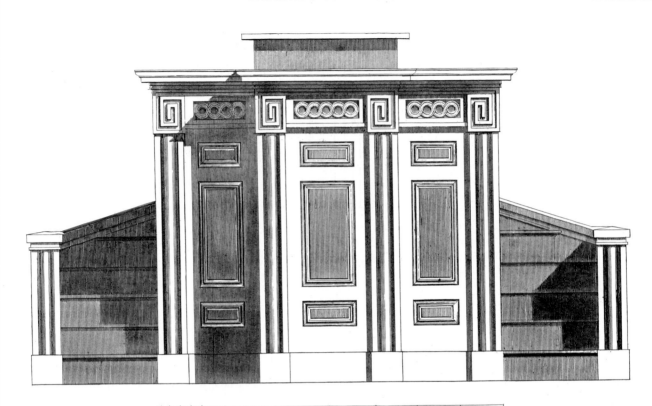

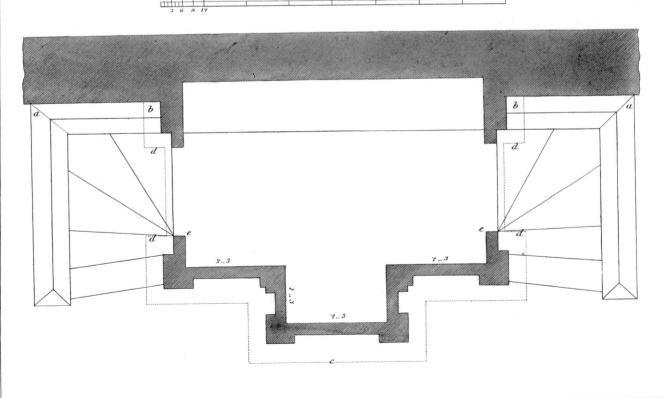

Fig. 1

2¼
5¾
1½
7½
1½
2
2½
2½
4⅜
4⅝
8¾
54½
8¾
6

23
16
16¾
7
11
1½
1¾
1½

a
b
c
42

Fig. 3
3½
3½
7
5
1 2
20

40 Parts

Fig. 1

Fig. 2

STAIRS.

PLATE LXII.

On this plate are a plan and elevation of a circular staircase, drawn from a scale of one inch to a foot. By an inspection of the plate, the method of drawing the elevation of a circular staircase will be clearly understood.

CHURCHES.

GENERAL REMARKS ON HOUSES ERECTED FOR PUBLIC WORSHIP.

THEIR character should harmonize particularly with the purpose for which they are designed; for the same proportions which would be beautiful in a room of a light or gay description, would be a defect in one of a solemn or devotional character. A building erected for public worship should therefore be so contrived as to produce in the beholder serious and devotional feelings. This effect is obtained by composing the building, generally, of large, bold, angular outlines, by continuing the entablatures and cornices unbroken over the columns and pilasters, and giving all the decorations, either of mouldings or sculpture, a large and grave appearance; excluding all ornaments composed of slender, curved, or winding outlines, which are expressive of lightness and gayety. The windows should be large, and so constructed as to admit the air to circulate freely throughout the house, without producing a glare of light; for a glare of light, and bright and gay colors, are opposed to solemnity in a house of worship. Ceilings are most appropriate when so arranged as to cause the greatest quantity of sound; and, if decorated at all, when divided into compartments, and ornamented by deep-sunk panels, surrounded by large plain fillets, or mouldings.

When columns are employed for the support of a gallery, they should be surmounted by an entablature, and the general proportions of the pedestal given to that part of the front of the gallery, above the entablature; and, as it is not usually convenient to make the plinth either very high or thick, it will be necessary to leave the upper edge square, or a little sloping. The face of the wainscot must be in a vertical line with the frieze of the entablature, and the panels deeply sunk, and surrounded by mouldings strongly marked, since, in the cornice, slender mouldings, viewed at the distance they must necessarily be, would appear indistinct; it will therefore be advisable to compose the cornice of a few bold parts.

The pulpit ought to partake of the character of the building in which it is erected. It may with propriety be made of mahogany, when pine is used for the finish of the other parts of the building; but the style of architecture, and decorations, must correspond with those of the house. Its height from the floor should be about seven feet, and the platform on which it stands should be raised at least two steps from the floor of the aisles, for the purpose of giving the congregation an opportunity of seeing the ordinances administered there. It has been a common practice to make two stair cases to a pulpit; a custom which cannot be justified by the rule of proportioning the means to the end, or any other, except that of uniformity. There does indeed seem to be a great impropriety in erecting two stair cases, where only one person is to ascend, and who cannot, of course, use but one at the same time ; but it is difficult to preserve the necessary uniformity without two stair cases ; and it will therefore be advisable to construct two, yet in such a manner as to make the least possible show, that they may appear as small in the composition as possible.

PLATE LXIII.

PULPIT.

On Plate LXIII. is a plan and elevation of a pulpit, drawn from a scale of one half an inch to a foot. Its height is seven feet above the platform on which it is to be placed. One end of the steps of each flight of stairs finishes against a buttress ; this buttress is formed like the pilasters, with the exception of the cap, which extends back to the wall *a a*, and by the wall, in a sloping direction, conforms to the inclination of the steps, until it butts against the pilasters at *b b*. The dotted line on the plan, at *c*, represents the projection of the cornice, the bedmould and corona of which profile against the pulpit on each side of both doors at *d d d d*. The crown moulding with its fillets continues across the doors, which are intended to be hung on the front side of the pulpit, *e e*, and to open inwards.

PLATE LXIV.

On this plate are designs for the entablature, pilasters and capping, drawn at one third of the full size. Divide the entire height into twenty-one equal parts ; give two to the diameter of the pilaster, two to the plinth, four to the height of the entablature, and fifteen to the height of the pilaster. The pilasters in this case are eight inches in diameter ; divide the diameter into forty equal parts, and by that scale draw all the mouldings.

Fig. 2 is a section of the pilaster at an external angle. Fig. 3 is a design for the capping to the buttress. Fig. 4 represents a section of the moulding for the panelling and a part of the panel, and also a part of the stile, at full size for practice. The guiloche in the panel is not to project beyond a vertical line of the frieze. In fig. 1, *a* should project four parts and two thirds from *b*, *c* should project three parts from *a*, and *d* should project three parts from *e*.

THE GRECIAN AND ROMAN ORDERS.

Remarks on these Orders, their Application and Fitness.

It is possible that many ingenious builders, who have, for a long time, rigidly adhered to the Roman system of the orders, particularly those who live at a distance from any of our large cities, and have not had opportunities for frequently visiting them, so as to witness with what a rapid progress the Grecian system has advanced beyond the Roman within the last fifteen or twenty years, may regard the general recommendation of the Grecian system of the orders as a whim of my own, and, without taking the trouble to give it a fair trial, reject it as an innovation on their former practice. Fearing this, and desiring to extend as far as possible the usefulness of the Grecian orders with all the details, I have thought it best to give the opinions and reasoning, on the Grecian and Roman orders, of Mr. James Elms, a distinguished English architect, who, in addition to a long and extensive practice, has had the advantage of visiting the most celebrated temples, both in Greece and Rome.

The Greek architects had no difficulties to contend with, in proportioning temples. According to Vitruvius, after the size of the front and number of columns have been determined upon, if six columns are in front, the whole front is to be divided into twenty-four and a half equal parts, without reckoning the projection of the bases of the two outer columns; the diameter of the column to be made equal to one of those parts, and the height equal to eight and a half diameters. He means, I suppose, to employ the Ionic order, as the Greeks always, when columns were employed on the flanks of their temples, used double the number, and one more, than they did on the front, counting the angular columns twice; so that, if six columns were employed in front, there would be thirteen along each of the sides. Where columns were not used on the flanks, it appears that the length bore the same proportion to the breadth of the building, as when they were used; and as they had not, as we have, to calculate for two or three stories in height, with windows in each to accommodate different sized rooms, stair cases, &c., we can suppose, that when the Doric order, in its full proportions, was employed on buildings of the size of the temple of Minerva at Athens, which was one hundred feet in breadth, and two hundred and twenty-five in length, with eight Doric columns on each front, and seventeen on each side, measuring six feet one inch in diameter, and, including capital, thirty-four feet two inches in height; the entrance doors on each front being twelve feet six inches in breadth, and twenty-eight feet eight inches in height; a building, moreover, constructed of the finest marble, and displaying the nicest workmanship; we may suppose, I say, in this case, that the proportions of this building, on so large a scale, would produce effects not to be surpassed by any alterations which could have been made in them.

But we have now to proportion buildings of a totally different character, and under much more embarrassing circumstances. If for public use, they are chiefly churches, buildings for the accommodation of our courts of justice, or banks.

If a church is to be erected, the committee, chosen for that purpose, will take care to instruct the architect not to make the building larger than is necessary for seating all their congregation. The architect is therefore under the necessity of making a gallery and two tiers of windows, unless, by making one tier of windows, he submits to the awkward appearance of the gallery crossing them. The increased size, and the additional expense, which would accrue by erecting porticos each side of the building, would forbid such an attempt; and the architect is confined to the front and rear of the house, where he may, indeed, show his taste and skill, by embellishing them with columns and entablatures, of the Greek proportions. The massive Doric may there often have its full proportions.

In a court house, there are generally two tiers of windows, and two stories—circumstances against adopting all the proportions of the Grecian temple; nevertheless, the architect may so construct such a building that it will produce a chaste and pleasing effect.

Banks, being usually built in our cities, and situated in the most crowded and business part of them, seldom show more than the front on the street, and, on account of the value of the land on which they are located, are often made three stories in height. This would forbid the front being embellished with columns, supporting a pediment, whose roof is in the same plane with the roof of the building; but if it should be only two stories in height, and completely insulated, then an opportunity is offered to the architect to decorate it with the Grecian orders and proportions.

All the Grecian buildings which have been accurately measured and transmitted to us, were erected for public purposes. Time has swept from us every vestige of their private houses, and it is impossible to ascertain, at the present day, whether or not the Grecian architects gave the same proportions to the Doric order, when used in their private dwellings, as when used in their temples. It is probable, however, that they were much lighter in the former case.

I see no propriety in making a Doric column, according to the Greek proportions, from four to six and a half diameters, when used in dwelling houses.

Take the case of a country house, constructed of wood, the front of which it is desired to decorate with a portico in the Grecian style. A house having such an embellishment would not be less than twenty-six feet in height. If it is to be of the Doric order, the example of the temple of Corinth would make the column four feet four inches in diameter,* and the entablature eight feet eight inches in height. No one could tolerate this proportion, since it would require the thickness of the column, at its base, to exceed the breadth of the doors and windows, and the entablature would cover one third of the front of the house.

Again, let us take the example of the portico of Philip, king of Macedon, which is one of the lightest of all the Grecian Dorics. By this example, the column would be three feet three quarters of an inch in diameter, and the entablature six feet one and a half inch in height; which is still much too large, especially if the columns are made of wood, as ours usually are.

Let us now take an example from the theatre of Marcellus, at Rome. This would make the column two feet nine inches in diameter, and the entablature five feet six inches in height.

No one, I think, will say that this last example is too light. If any thing different is preferable, it is to make the column two feet six inches. I therefore repeat what I have before said, that the

* I leave out the fractional parts.

general proportions of the Roman Doric orders come nearer to our practice in private buildings than the Grecian proportions. The Greeks and Romans did not differ essentially in their general proportions of the Ionic and Corinthian orders.

It will be seen, by turning to page 16, on which is a table of the proportions of all the Grecian Dorics which have been accurately measured, that the column in the temple of Corinth is four diameters and four minutes in height, and the column in the portico of Philip, six diameters thirty-two and a half minutes in height; making a difference of two diameters twenty-eight and a half minutes in the height of the columns of these two examples. The capitals, likewise, of these examples, differ as widely as the columns; that in the temple of Corinth being in height twenty-four and a quarter minutes, and projecting sixteen minutes, while that of the portico of Philip is in height fourteen and one third minutes, and projects six and a quarter minutes. The contour of the echinus in the latter capital is a straight line, and the contour of that at Corinth is elliptical.

It seems to be supposed, by many persons, that the Grecian orders must be executed without any deviations from the original examples. Of such persons I would inquire, what example they would choose; for it is a singular fact, that no two can be found which agree, either in their general proportions or in their details. To those acquainted with this fact, it is needless to urge the impropriety of binding one's self to a servile imitation of the general proportions of any of those examples, unless they happen to suit our purpose.

I do believe, however, that it is wise in us to study all the systems of architecture, in particular those of Greece and Rome, and, in determining the general proportions of a building, to endeavor to proportion the means to the end ; but, in the details, I believe no one, who thoroughly understands the two systems, can hesitate for a moment in giving his decided preference to the Grecian.

I will give here the above-mentioned extracts from **Mr. Elmes**, which, I think, will be read with interest, and, I hope, to advantage. They are taken from his Lectures, published in **1821**.

"The great superiority of the Greeks in architecture is to be traced to causes similar to those which occasioned their pre-eminence in every thing else ; namely, a deep investigation into first principles ; an accurate perception of the *elements* of all that they attempted to execute.

"A similar investigation, and a similar perception or knowledge, and nothing else, will produce the like effects in our country and in our times.

"To the Greeks, and to them alone, let the student look for grandeur of composition, and, indeed, for all the laws of architecture, painting and sculpture.

"The grand divisions of the architecture of Greece are, first, the three orders of columns, technically called *the orders :* secondly, the several orders of temples, or their sacred edifices ; and, thirdly, the various methods of intercolumniations, or manner of regulating the distances of columns.

"It is these great or primary divisions, and their due observance, which entitle the architecture of the Greeks to the dignified epithet of the *wisdom of the orders.*

"Every order is composed of primary and divisional parts, which differ in each of the orders, as will presently be described.

"Every column, except the Doric, has three parts; the base, the shaft, and the capital. The lowest or thickest part of the shaft is used by architects as the universal standard whence all the measures which regulate and determine heights and projections are taken.

"The bases of the various orders differ from each other in their essential parts, and even among themselves, in non-essentials, although not in character. The base of a column is composed of a series of mouldings encircling the bottom diameter according to its order.

"The Doric has no base. The Ionic differs in various specimens; but that which has been the most used for this order is called the Attic base, and is composed of a cubical plinth, on which are a circular torus, a fillet, a scotia, and a compound moulding called an astragal, consisting of a small torus and two fillets, one above and the other below. A small cavetto, or hollow, connects the upper fillet, which is somewhat larger than a diameter, to the lower extremity of the shaft.

"From this simple and beautiful base all the others appear to have emanated, as it contains the component members and leading characteristics of them all. It has also been more universally used than any of the others, having been borrowed from its Ionian proprietor by the Corinthian, and even occasionally by the Roman Doric.

"Some of the Greek, or true Ionic bases, differ from the Attic in their arrangements, but are generally inferior where the difference is essential.

"The Corinthian base consists of a plinth, a torus, a fillet, then a large scotia, next a fillet, sometimes two beads, then a second and

smaller scotia, and the concluding astragal, fillets, and usual hollow
on the top to connect it with the shaft.

"The Composite base differs so little from the Corinthian, where
the Attic base is not used, that it is not worth detailing.

"Having thus defined the lower division of the column, its base,
our next step will be to the shaft. The shaft of a column is that
columnar conical body which is situated between the base and the
capital. In some examples, it is plain, in others, fluted, or divided
into perpendicular circular channels, which are differently formed,
and variously divided, in the different orders. In the Doric, that is,
the true Doric, they are formed without intervening fillets, and are
called by workmen arris flutes. Such are Doric flutes, which should
never be used to any other order, nor should any other kind of fluting
ever be applied to the Doric order. These rules are sanctioned by
first principles, and the examples of the Greeks, and violated by the
Romans, the modern Italians, and the Anglo-Italian architects of the
present day.

"The flutings of the Ionic and Corinthian shafts are differently
executed. Between each flute there is a fillet or part of the shaft
left uncut, of half its width, and the flutes are channelled in equal to
half their width, forming semicircles on their plan. These are also
often fluted only two thirds of the way down, and then the lower
third is carved to resemble a circular staff placed in the flutes and
rounded on the top.

"The next and concluding portion of the column is the capital,
which differs, according to the order to which it belongs. The
capital is the most striking part of an order, and, to common ob-
servers, is the portion by which they best judge the name of an
order. In the pure, that is, the Greek system of classical architec-

ture, every other part of an order bears its character as completely as the capitals; but in the Roman and modern systems, they are huddled, mixed and perverted, in a manner destructive to good taste and correct classification.

"The capital of the Doric order agrees in character in all the ancient examples, although it differs in minor parts, which difference is specific, and does not detract from the generic characteristics of the order : therefore the following general description is applicable to all.

"The Doric capital is divided into three principal parts—the abacus, the echinus, and the annulets. The abacus is the superior member or covering of the capital, and appertains to each of the three orders, but it assumes a different and characteristic form in each. In the Doric and Ionic, the abacus is square in its plan, plain in the Doric, and moulded in the Ionic; and in the Corinthian, each face is hollowed into a circular, and (with the exception of the example in the portico at Athens, called the Poekile) cut off at the angles.

"The abacus of the Doric capital is a parallelopipedon, or unequal cube, varying from ten to twelve minutes, or about the sixth part of the bottom diameter, in height, in the best examples. Immediately under the abacus is the large elliptico-circular member, called the echinus, the outline of which resembles a chestnut. The echinus, in the finest specimens of the order, is either elliptical or hyperbolical in its perpendicular outline, but never circular ; and, with the annulets under it, is the same height as the abacus.

"The annulets, as their name imports, are three rings, or circular fillets, under the echinus, falling off under each other perpendicularly, like an inverted flight of steps, and partaking of the general outline of the echinus in the arrangement of its angles.

"In many examples, at about thirty minutes below the top of the abacus, is a channel sunk round the shaft, as if to determine the size of the capital, situated in the place of the Roman hypotrachelion, or necking, whether the shaft be fluted or plain.

"In no instance is the superiority of the Grecian style of architecture over the Roman more apparent than when viewed comparatively, in this order. To the beautiful and characteristic abacus of the true Doric, the Romans have added the moulded cymatium and fillet on the top. For the chaste simplicity and elegant outline of the echinus, they have substituted the clumsy and tasteless ovolo, which they even have often spoiled by carving. For the annulet, they often substitute an astragal, or a bead and fillet. For the delicate and effective channelled hypotrachelion, they bolster round the shaft the colarino of the Corinthian ; and, to complete the absurdity, leaves have even been added in the part between the necking and the under moulding of the capital, which Palladio, oddly enough, calls the frieze of the capital. To its beautifully proportioned shaft they have added several diameters in height. For its conical outline, they have substituted the swelling shaft ; and for the shallow arris flutings of the original, the semicircularly hollowed flutes and wide fillets of the other orders have not seldom been misapplied.

"I shall now proceed to the investigation and description of the Ionic order. The Ionic capital is divided into two principal or leading features, the abacus and the volutes. The abacus is a right-angled parallelogram, nearly square on its plan, and moulded on its perpendicular sides, or edges, sometimes with a cymatium, sometimes with an echinus. The volutes are two spiral mouldings on each side of the front, perpendicular to the horizon, alike on two faces, and the other two profiles or sides alike in themselves, but differing from the front; the extremities of each are the same distance from the centre of the column. Each spiral, or volute, has the same number of volutions, or spirals, which are differently connected by mouldings, passing between and behind them, round the shaft of the column.

"One of the most beautiful examples of simple dignity found in this order, or perhaps in any other, is that of the small Ionic temple on the banks of the river Illyssus, at Athens.

"Another fine and more embellished example of the Ionic order, is taken from the beautiful temple of Minerva Polias, at Priene, in Ionia; the architect of which was Pytheus, who, requiring an enriched order, did not, like the Romans, corrupt the Doric with misplaced ornaments, but rejected it entirely, and composed this elegant specimen upon the pure elements of the ancient order. The small projection of the cymatium, or upper moulding of the cornice, and its great height, are beautiful, and well adapted to receive its ornaments, as it is less obscured by the shadow of the concave and convex parts of the moulding. The dentils are introduced in the bed-mould of the cornice with great propriety and effect, as their bold and singular projection relieves them completely from each other. The architrave is well proportioned; but, having three fasciæ instead of two, it encroaches too much upon the Corinthian.

"The capital is an elegant and embellished variation of that from the Illyssus; it is more enriched, without destroying the harmony and elegance of its proportions, and the spirals of the volutes are elegantly and tastefully drawn.

"The hem, or border, of this capital, from volute to volute, with its delicate fillet resting on the grandly designed ovolo, connecting with a graceful curve the spirals of the volute, seems to keep them in their situations, and greatly conduces to the beauty of the capital.

"Our next and last step, in the description of the orders, is to the Corinthian. This is the richest and most embellished, and is, as it were, the seal and completion of them all.

"This order, though the most embellished, is yet the most simple and easy to use in either colonnades or porticos, having neither the difficulty of the triglyphs of the Doric, nor the dissimilar faces of the Ionic, which require much skill to adapt in angle columns.

"The principal examples of the Corinthian order, now remaining in Italy and Greece, do not differ from each other so essentially in character as either the Doric or the Ionic.

"The Corinthian order, as used in the Pantheon, at Rome, is, although rather plain, of beautiful proportions: it is chaste, correct, and an excellent model for imitation and study. Another very fine example is found in the three columns of the Campo Vaccino, at Rome, supposed to be the remains of the temple of Jupiter Stator. The elegance and beauty of this example, particularly the capital, its graceful form, and the delicacy of its ornaments, render it one of the most complete examples now existing of the Corinthian order.

"Another fine specimen of this order is that of the temple of Vesta, or the Sybil, at Tivoli, near Rome. Yet no less to be admired is the order of the Choragic monument of Lysicrates, near Athens, called by some travellers the lantern of Demosthenes.

"Having extolled the architecture of the Greeks above that of the Romans, in a manner beyond what the admirers of the Roman style may approve, permit me to repeat, by way of explanation, that it was not in costliness or magnitude, that the mighty genius of the Greeks developed itself, so much as in *invention*, in *taste*, in *beauty*, in *refinement*, and in leaving to posterity the *best models for imitation.* These qualities have given this gifted people their deserved pre-eminence over all their imitators or competitors.

"No remains of architecture or sculpture are to be found in Greece but what are canons of art, while Rome possesses more to corrupt the taste of the young architect than all its excellences can counterbalance. It is, therefore, to the rules, the forms, the proportions, the taste of the former, that the attention of the student should be perpetually recalled.

"The three essential and distinct qualities in architecture are *strength, grace* and *richness.* The three orders of the Greeks possess all these requisites, and the five anomalous orders of the Romans possess no more. The aforesaid qualities are the landmarks, the boundaries, the north and south poles of the art. The Doric displays the first-mentioned quality of strength ; the Ionic, the second, of grace ; and the Corinthian, the third, of richness. The Corinthian is the *maximum,* uniting beautiful simplicity and florid decoration ; while the Doric possesses pure simplicity, plainness and robust strength ; and the Ionic is the connecting link between the two.

"The orders and styles of architecture are but the *means ;* to build with good sense, propriety and taste, is the *end.*

"Ancient examples, selected with judgment and pure taste ; adapted, with the latitude of genius, to modern necessities ; combined with the scientific inventions of modern construction ; and perfected by study and practice ; are the best schools of true architecture.

"The Roman Doric order has been so altered and abused, by various architects, since the decline of Grecian purity, that some examples hardly appear to belong to the same order. This order is by Palladio restored and compounded from all the best antique specimens found by him in Rome : his column is purer in style than any single ancient remain.   The bed moulding, or under part of the cornice, however, is too complex and enriched for the simplicity and manly character of the order.   The frieze is divided as he found the best remains in ancient Rome, and the triglyphs are consequently misdivided ; the architrave has two faces, and the whole entablature too small a proportion of height.   The capital is also overloaded with ornament, the abacus is destroyed by the addition of mouldings ; the echinus is converted to a quadrant ; and the graceful channelling of the Greek hypotrachelion is omitted, to make room for a clumsy necking, belonging to any order *but* the Doric.   He has also added a base to the shaft, and omitted the beautiful mutules which support the corona over every triglyph and metope of the Greek original.

"The next order in the Roman system is their Ionic, which differs almost as much in detail as the Doric.   In its leading character, the volutes, however, it has not been so violated as the Doric.

"The first specimen to which I beg leave to call your attention, is from the temple of Fortuna Virilis, at Rome, an excellent restoration of which, in all its details, may be found in Palladio's work on the ancient temples of Rome.   Its order is undoubtedly the best to be found in Rome, and resembles the one of the theatre of Marcellus, but will not bear comparison with the beautiful Greek original, whose name it usurps.

"It remains for the student to inquire from which source, Roman or Greek, he can draw the most graceful proportions of the Ionic order.   In the Roman specimens, their overloaded cornices, their ill-proportioned entablatures, their vulgar profiles, and the broken spiral lines of their volutes, render them, in my opinion, utterly unfit for models."

GLOSSARY OF ARCHITECTURAL TERMS.

A.

Aaron's Rod; an ornamental figure representing a rod with a serpent entwined about it, and called by some, though improperly, the Caduceus of Mercury.

Abacus; the upper member of a capital of a column, serving as a kind of crown-piece in the Grecian Doric, and a collection of members or mouldings in the other orders.

Abutment; a pier, upon which the extremity of an arch rests.

Accessories; in architectural composition, those parts, or ornaments, either designed or accidental, which are not apparently essential to the use and character of a building.

Acropolis; from the Greek; the highest part of a city, the citadel or fortress.

Acroteria; small pedestals placed on the apex and two sides of a pediment. They sometimes support statues.

Ægricanes; sculptures representing the heads and skulls of rams; commonly used as a decoration of ancient altars, friezes, &c.

Ætoma; a pediment, or the tympanum of a pediment.

Aile, or *Aisle;* a walk in a church on the sides of the nave; the wings of a choir.

Alcove; a recess, or part of a chamber, separated by an estrade, or partition of columns, and other corresponding ornaments.

Amphiprostyle; an order of temples among the Greeks, having columns in the back, as well as the front.

Alto-relievo, or *High-relief;* that kind or portion of sculpture, which projects so much from the surface to which it is attached as to appear nearly insulated. It is therefore used in comparison with *Mezzo-relievo,* or *Mean-relief,* and in opposition to *Basso-relievo,* or *Low-relief.*

Amphitheatre; a spacious edifice, of a circular or oval form, in which the combats and shows of antiquity were exhibited.

Ancones; the carved key-stone of arches.

Angle-rafter; in carpentry, otherwise *Hip-rafter;* see *Hip.*

Angular capital; the modern Ionic, or Scammozian capital, which is formed alike on all the four faces, so as to return at the angles of the building.

Annulet; a small square moulding, commonly used to connect the others.

Antæ; small projections, in Grecian architecture, from the wall, to receive the entablature from the columns of a portico, and having bases and capitals different from the columns.

Apophyge; the curve connecting the upper fillet of the base, or under one of the capital, with the cylindrical part of the shaft.

Aræostyle; a manner of intercolumniation, in which all the columns are distant from each other about four diameters.

Arcade; an aperture in a wall, with an arched head. It also signifies a range of apertures with arched heads.

Arch; a part of a building supported at its extremities only, and concave towards the earth or horizon.

Architectonic; something endowed with the power and skill of building, or calculated to assist the architect.

Architrave; the undermost principal division of an entablature.

Astragal; a small moulding, semicircular in profile.

B.

Back; generally that side of an object which is opposite to the face, or breast : but the back of a handrail is the upper side of it; that of a rafter is the upper side of it, in the sloping plane of one side of a roof.

Back-shutters, or *Back-flaps;* additional breadths hinged to the front-shutters, for completely closing the aperture, when the window is to be shut.

Balcony (from the French *balcon*); an open gallery, projecting from the front of a building, and commonly constructed of iron or wood.

Baluster; a small kind of column or pillar, belonging to a balustrade.

Balustrade; a range of balusters, supporting a cornice, and used as a parapet or screen, for concealing a roof, or other object.

Band; a square member in a profile.

Base; the lower division of a column. In the Greek Doric there is no base.

Battlement; see *Parapet.*

Bay-window; a window projecting from the front, in two or more planes, and not forming the segment of a circle.

Bed-mouldings; the mouldings below the corona in a cornice.

Belfry, anciently the *campanile;* the part of a steeple in which the bells are hung.

Belvidere; a turret, look-out, or observatory, commanding a fine prospect, and generally very ornamental.

Boultin; a name for the echinus.

Bow-window; a window forming the segment of a circle.

Broach (in Gothic architecture); a spire, or polygonal pyramid, whether of stone or timber.

Bracket (in Gothic architecture); a projection to sustain a statue, or other ornament, and sometimes supporting the ribs of a roof.

Buttress (in Gothic architecture); a projection on the exterior of a wall, to strengthen the piers and resist the pressure of the arches within.

C.

Cabling; cylindrical pieces let into the lower part of the flutes of columns.

Caduceus; an emblem or attribute of Mercury; a rod entwined by two-winged serpents.

Caisson; a name for sunk panels of geometrical forms.

Campana; the body of the Corinthian capital.

Campanæ, or *Campanula,* or *Guttæ;* the drops of the Doric architrave.

Canopy (in Gothic architecture); the ornamental dripstone of an arch. It is usually of the ogee form.

Canted (in Gothic architecture); any part of a building having its angles cut off, is said to be canted.

Capital; the upper division of a column, or pillar.

Cartouch; the square blocks under the eaves of a house.

Cant-moulding; a bevelled surface, neither perpendicular to the horizon, nor to the vertical surface to which it may be attached.

Cap (in joinery); the uppermost of an assemblage of parts, as the capital of a column, the cornice of a door, &c.

Caryatidæ, or *Caryatides;* so called from the Caryatides, a people of Caria; an order of columns or pilasters, under the figures of women dressed in long robes, after the manner of the Carian people, and serving to support an entablature. This order is called the *Caryatic.*

Case of a door; the frame in which the door is hung.

Catacomb; a subterraneous place for the interment of the dead.

Cavetto; one of the regular mouldings of Roman architecture, hollowed in the form of a quadrant of a circle.

Chancel; the communion place, or that part of a Christian church between the altar and balustrade which encloses it.

Chantry; a small chapel on the side of a church.

Cincture; a ring or fillet surrounding the top and bottom of a shaft, with which it is connected by the apophyge.

Circus; a spacious building in which equestrian exercises are exhibited.

Coin, or *Quoin;* the corner or angle made by the two surfaces of a stone or brick building, whether external or internal.

Colonnade; a range of columns, whether attached or insulated, and supporting an entablature.

Column; according to the best method of describing it, a column is a frustum of a very elongated parabola, and circular in its plan. It consists (in Greek and Roman architecture) of three parts, viz. the base, the shaft, and the capital.

Composite order; one of the Roman orders of architecture.

Conge; a moulding consisting of a simple curve, whether bending outwards, as the ovolo or swelling conge, or inwards, as the cavetto or hollow conge.

Conservatory; a superior kind of greenhouse for valuable plants, &c., arranged in beds of earth, with ornamental borders.

Console; a bracket, or projecting body, shaped like a curve of contrary flexure, scrolled at the ends, and serving to support a cornice, bust, vase, or other ornament. Consoles are also called, according to their form, ancones or trusses, mutules and modillions.

Continued; uninterrupted, unbroken, as a continued attic, pedestal, &c., not broken by pilasters or columns.

Contour; a French word for Outline.

Coping; the stones laid on the top of a wall, to strengthen and defend it from injury.

Corbeils; carved work representing baskets filled with flowers or fruit, and used as a finish to some elegant part of a building. This word is sometimes used to express the bell or vase of the Corinthian capital.

Corinthian order; one of the orders of architecture.

Cornice; a crowning; any moulded projection which crowns or finishes the part to which it is attached.

Cornucopia; the horn of plenty, represented in sculpture under the figure of a large horn, out of which issue fruits, flowers, grain, &c.

Corona; the upper member of a cornice, in Greek and Roman architecture.

Corridor; a gallery or passage, in large buildings, which leads to distant apartments.

Counter-forts; projections of masonry from a wall, at certain regular distances, for strengthening it or resisting a pressure.

Coupled columns; those disposed in pairs, so as to form a narrow and wide interval alternately.

Crosettes; in decoration, the trusses or consoles on the flanks of the architrave, under the cornice.

Crown; the uppermost member of a cornice, including the corona, &c; of an arch, its most elevated line or point.

Cupola; a dome; the hemispherical summit of a building.

Cusp (in Gothic architecture); a name for the segments of circles forming the trefoil, quatrefoil, &c.

Cyma, Cymatium; the cyma is of two kinds : the cyma-recta, a moulding hollowed at the top and swelling beneath, generally called cymatium ; and the cyma-reversa, or ogee, which is swelled above and hollowed beneath.

D.

Dentils; small square projections used in the cornices of several of the Roman orders, and in the Grecian Ionic.

Diastyle; a manner of intercolumniation in which the columns are three diameters apart.

Die of a pedestal; the part comprehended between the base and cornice.

Ditriglyph; having two triglyphs over an intercolumn.

Dome; a concave ceiling, commonly hemispherical.

Doric order; one of the orders of architecture.

Dormant, or *Dormer Window* (in Gothic architecture); a window set upon the slope of a roof or spire.

Drops; in ornamental architecture, small pendent cylinders, or frustums of cones attached to a surface vertically, with the upper ends touching a horizontal surface, as in the cornice of the Doric order.

Drum, or *Vase, of the Corinthian and Composite capitals;* the solid part to which the foliage and stalks, or ornaments, are attached.

Dye; the plain part of a pedestal, between the base and cornice.

E.

Eaves ; the margin or edge of a roof overhanging the walls.

Echinus ; a moulding in the Roman orders, consisting of the quadrant of a circle turned outwards ; in the Greek, it is composed of one of the conic sections.

Embattled ; a building with a parapet, having embrasures, and therefore resembling a battery, or castle.

Encarpus ; the festoons on a frieze ; see *Festoon.*

Entablature ; the horizontal part of an order, supported by the columns.

Entail (in Gothic architecture); delicate carving.

Entasis ; the swelling of a column.

Epistylium ; or *architrave* of the entablature.

Eustyle ; the manner of intercolumniation in which the columns are distant two diameters and a quarter.

F

Façade ; the face or front of a building.

Falling moulds ; in joinery, the two moulds which are to be applied to the vertical sides of the railpiece, in order to form the back and under surface of the rail, and finish the squaring.

Fane, Phane, Vane (in Gothic architecture); a plate of metal, usually cut into some fantastic form, and turning on a pivot, to determine the course of the wind.

Fascia ; a band or fillet. This term is usually employed to denote the flat members into which the architrave is divided.

Fastigium ; see *Pediment.*

Festoon ; a carved ornament resembling a wreath, attached at both ends, and falling in the middle.

Fillet ; see *Annulet.*

Flutings ; vertical channels on the shafts of columns.

Flyers ; steps of which the treads are all parallel.

Fret ; a species of ornament commonly composed of straight grooves or channelures at right angles to each other. The labyrinth fret has many turnings, or angles, but in all cases the parts are parallel and perpendicular to each other.

Frieze ; the member of an entablature between the architrave and cornice.

Fust ; the shaft of a column.

G.

Glyphs ; the channels in the triglyphs of the Doric frieze.

Gola ; see *Ogee.*

Gothic ; a peculiar style of architecture, distinct from either the Grecian or Roman.

Gorge ; see *Cavetto.*

Greek orders of architecture ; the Doric, Ionic, and Corinthian. See these names respectively.

Griffin, or *Griffon ;* a fabulous animal, sacred to Apollo, and mostly represented with the head and wings of an eagle, and the body, legs and tail of a lion.

Groin ; the diagonal line formed by the intersection of two vaults in a roof.

Groined ceiling ; a cradling constructed of ribs.

Grotesque ; the light, gay and beautiful style of ornament practised by the ancient Romans in the decoration of their palaces, baths, villas, &c.

Guiloches ; an ancient ornament composed of fillets, which cross and recross each other, and generally encompass a plain or ornamented roset.

Guttæ ; small cones, representing drops, placed in the soffit of the mutules, and under the triglyphs in the Doric entablature.

H.

Hall ; a word commonly denoting a mansion, or large public building, as well as the large room at the entrance.

Hyperthyron ; the lintel of a doorway.

Hypotrachelion ; the neck of a capital.

I.

Impost ; any combination of mouldings serving as the capital or cornice of a pier.

Intercolumniation ; the distance between two columns.

Insulated ; standing alone, or detached from any contiguous building.

Ionic order ; one of the orders of architecture.

J.

Jambs ; the vertical sides of an aperture, as of doors, windows, &c.

K.

Key-stone ; the centre or highest stone in an arch. It is frequently larger than the rest, and ornamented with sculpture.

L.

Labyrinth ; a building, tne numerous passages and perplexing windings of which, render the escape from it difficult, and almost impossible. Hence, *Labyrinth fret ;* a fret with many turnings, which was a favorite ornament of the ancients.

Lacunariæ, or *Lacunars ;* panels or coffers formed on the ceilings of apartments, and sometimes on the soffits of coronæ in the Ionic, Corinthian and Composite orders.

Lantern ; a turret raised above the roof, with windows round the sides, and constructed for lighting an apartment beneath.

Larmier ; see *Corona.*

Lintel ; the horizontal piece which covers the opening of a door or window.

List ; see *Fillet.*

M.

Mechanical powers ; such implements or machines as are used for raising greater weights, or overcoming greater resistances, than could be effected by the natural strength without them.

Medallion ; a circular tablet, ornamented with embossed or carved figures, bustos, &c.

Metope ; the space between two triglyphs in the Doric frieze. It is frequently decorated with sculpture.

Mezzanino ; a low story between two floors.

Minaret ; a Turkish steeple with a balcony.

Minute ; the sixtieth part of the diameter of a column.

Modillion ; a projection under the corona of the richer orders, resembling a bracket.

Module ; the semi-diameter of a column at the foot of a shaft.

Mono-triglyph ; having only one triglyph between two adjoining columns : the general practice in the Grecian Doric.

Mouldings ; the smaller parts of architecture, whether Roman or Grecian, which are shaped in regular forms. They are so called from being worked with a mould.

Mutale ; those projections in the Doric cornice supposed to represent the ends of rafters.

N.

Nave ; the body of a church, reaching from the choir or chancel to the principal door.

Neck of a capital ; the space between the channelures and the annulets of the Grecian Doric capital ; in the Roman Doric, the space between the astragal and annulet.

Newel ; in a circular staircase, the centre round which the steps ascend.

Niche ; a cavity in a wall, to receive a statue, or other ornament.

O.

Obelisk ; a quadrangular pyramid, high and slender, raised as a monument or ornament, and commonly charged with inscriptions and ornaments.

Odeum ; among the ancients, a place for the rehearsal of music and other particular purposes.

Ogee ; a moulding of two members, one concave, the other convex. It is otherwise called a cymatium.

Orlo ; the plinth of a column or pedestal.

Ovolo ; see *Echinus.*

Orthography ; an elevation showing all the parts of a building in true proportion.

P.

Pagoda, or *Pagod ;* an Indian temple common in Hindostan and the countries to the east. These structures, dedicated to idolatry, are mostly of stone, square, not very lofty, without windows, and crowned with a cupola.

Panel ; a compartment enclosed by mouldings.

Parapet ; a low wall round the roof of a building.

Pavilion ; a kind of turret or building usually insulated, and contained under a single roof; sometimes square and sometimes in the form of a dome ; thus called from the resemblance of its roof to a tent.

Pedestal; a square body of stone, or other material, raised to sustain a column, statue, &c. It is therefore the base, or lowest part, of an order of columns. A square pedestal is that of which the height and width are equal.

Pediment; an ornament, properly of a low triangular figure, crowning the front of a building.

Pentastyle; an edifice having five columns in front.

Periptere; a building encompassed with columns, which form a kind of aisle around it.

Piazza; a portico, or covered walk, supported by arches.

Pilaster; a pillar of a rectangular plan.

Pillar; a column of an irregular make, not formed according to rules, but of arbitrary proportions; free or insulated in every part, and always deviating from the measures of regular columns. This is the distinction of the pillar from the column. A square pillar is sometimes called a pier.

Pinnacle; the top or roof of a building, terminating in a point.

Planceer; see *Soffit.*

Platband; a square member of slight projection.

Plinth; the square solid under the base of a column, pedestal or wall.

Porch; the kind of vestibule at the entrance of temples, halls, churches, &c.

Portico; an entablature supported by columns, and surmounted by a pediment.

Post and Railing; an open wooden fence, consisting of posts and rails only.

Profile; the contour of the parts composing an order.

Pronaos; an ancient name for a porch to a temple or other spacious building.

Proscenium; in a theatre, the stage, or the front of it.

Prostyle; having columns in front only.

Pycnostyle; a manner of intercolumniation of one diameter and a half.

Pyramid; a solid figure, having its base triangular, square, or polygonal, and terminating in a **point at top.**

Q.

Quadra; any square border or frame encompassing a basso-relievo, panel, &c.

Quirk mouldings; the convex parts of Grecian mouldings, where they recede at the top, and form a re-entrant angle with the soffit which covers the moulding.

Quoin, external or internal; the name is particularly applied to the stones at the corners of brick buildings. When these stand out beyond the brick work, with edges chamfered, they are called *Rustic Quoins.*

R.

Raiser; a board set on edge under the fore side of a step or stair.

Raking Moulding; a moulding whose arrises are inclined to the horizon in any given angle.

Ramp; in handrailing, a concavity on the upper side, formed over risers, or over a half or quarter space, by a sudden rise of the steps above.

Reglet, or *Riglet;* a flat, narrow moulding, used chiefly in compartments and panels, to separate the parts or members, and to form knots or frets, &c.

Revels, pronounced *Reveals;* the vertical retreating surface of an aperture, as the two vertical sides between the front of the wall and the windows or door frame.

Roman, or *Composite order.*

Rose; an ornament in the form of a rose, found chiefly in cornices, friezes, &c.

Rotundo, or *Rotunda;* a common name for any circular building.

Rudenture; the figure of a rope, or of a staff, whether plain or carved, with which a third part of the fluting of columns is frequently filled up. It is sometimes called cabling: hence the columns are said to be cabled, or rudented.

Rustic; a manner of masonry in which the stones are indented at their angles; also stones left rough.

S.

Saloon; a spacious, lofty and elegant hall, or apartment, vaulted at top, and generally having two ranges of windows.

Section of a Building; a representation of it, as vertically divided into two parts, so as to exhibit the construction of the interior.

Sesspool, or *Cesspool;* a deep hole, or well, under the mouth of a drain, for the reception of sediment, &c. by which the drain might be choked.

Sewer; a common drain, or conductor for conveying foul water, &c.

Shaft; the part of a column between the base and capital.

Shank; a name for the flat space between the channels in the Doric triglyph.

Socle, or *Zocle;* a square piece, broader than it is high, placed under the bases of pedestals, &c. to support vases, and other ornaments. As there is a continued pedestal, so there is also a continued socle. See *Pedestal.*

Soffita, or *Soffit;* any timber ceiling formed of cross beams of flying cornices, the square compartments or panels of which are enriched with sculpture or painting. *Soffit* also means the under side of an architrave, and that of the corona, or drip, &c.; also the horizontal undersides of the heads of apertures, as of doors and windows.

Sphinx; a favorite ornament of Egyptian architecture, representing the monster, half woman and half beast, said to have been born of Typhon and Echidna.

Spire; a slender pyramid of a polygonal plan.

Squaring handrails; the method of cutting a plank to the form of a rail for a staircase, so that all the vertical sections may be rectangles.

String-board; in stairing, a board placed next to the well-hole, and terminating the ends of the steps.

Stylobata; see *Pedestal.*

Systyle; an intercolumniation of two diameters.

T.

Tænia; the term for the fillet separating the frieze from the architrave in the Doric order.

Talon; a French term, either for the astragal or cyma-reversa.

Terrace; an elevated area for walking upon, and sometimes meaning a balcony.

Tetrastyle; having four columns in front.

Torus; a large moulding, semicircular in profile, used in bases.

Tread of a step; the horizontal part of it.

Triglyph; the ornament in the Doric frieze supposed to represent the end of beams.

Tripod; a three-legged seat, from which the priests of antiquity delivered their oracles, and frequently represented in architectural ornaments.

Trophy; an ornament representing the trunk of a tree, supporting military weapons, colors, &c.

Tuscan order; one of the Roman orders of architecture.

Tympanum; the space within a pediment. It is sometimes adorned with sculpture.

V.

Valley; the internal angle of two inclined sides of a roof.

Vase; a name for the bell, or naked form of the Corinthian capital, on which the leaves are disposed.

Vault; an arched roof. When more than a semicircle, they are called *surmounted,* and when less, *surbased* vaults.

Venetian door; a door lighted on each side.

Venetian window; a window having three separate apertures.

Volute; the scroll which distinguishes the Ionic capital.

W.

Wreathed columns; such as are twisted in the form of a screw. Not now used.

Z.

Zocle; see *Socle.*

Zophorus; see *Frieze.*

Zystos; among the ancients, a portico or aisle of unusual length, commonly appropriated to gymnastic exercises.